THE GROWING FAMILY SERIES

The Fussy Baby

How to Bring Out the Best in Your High-Need Child

D1509059

THE GROWING FAMILY SERIES

The Fussy Baby

How to Bring Out the Best in Your High-Need Child

William Sears, MD & Martha Sears, RN

La Leche League International
Schaumburg, Illinois

Acknowledgements

Our thanks go out to the hundreds of parents who have shared their stories and contributed to this book and to our children who with their unique individual temperaments have made us richer human beings. A note of appreciation goes to the hundreds of high-need babies whom Bill has personally attended in his pediatric practice and from whom we both have learned much.

First edition, July 1985
Revised edition, May 2002
07 06 05 04 03 02 7 6 5 4 3 2 1
ISBN 0912500-88-3   SEP 8 - 2004
Library of Congress Catalog Card Number 2001091628

Printed in the United States of America

Book and cover design: Digital Concepts, LLC
Photo credits: Cover photos by David Arendt; photos on pages 3, 23, 122 by Subhadra Tidball; pages 5, 9, 21, 53, 59, 94, 95, 108, 109, 116, 120, 130, 138, 140, 143, 154, 157, 168, 183, 184, 187, 193 by David Arendt; page 14 by Judy Torgus; pages 33, 49, 97, 117, 123, 129, 130 by Dale Pfeiffer; page 36 by Mary Ann Cahill; page 43 by Kaye Lowman; page 96 by Paul Torgus; page 106 courtesy of Crowncrafts; page 115 by Gretchen Shields; page 181 by Betsy Liotus.

Contents

Foreword

I've spent many hours rocking, walking, dancing, and singing to a baby who just couldn't get comfortable or fall asleep. The fussiest of my babies was my sixth. By then I was comfortable with babies and had learned how to be an excellent baby soother. I thought I knew exactly how to calm and cuddle any baby. It was quite a shock when this baby arched her back and screamed even though I had nursed her, checked her diaper and other clothing to see if anything was hurting her, nursed her again, wrapped, then unwrapped her, and tried to feed her yet again. Nothing seemed to help. She just continued to scream while I danced and walked with her, took her outside, and then came back in again. It was a frustrating time of life for us both. She was healthy, the doctor assured me again and again, so I couldn't understand what was the matter. Why was she so fussy?

Dr. Bill Sears has written this book to help parents through trying times like these. He explains that a baby's cry is one of the loudest of all human sounds and that it activates a strong response in everyone within earshot. It is a sound that I, as well as most parents, hurried to quiet. But when our attempts to comfort a baby don't work we become frustrated, angry, and miserable.

Dr. Sears details ways for parents to interact with fussy babies. By describing them as high-need babies, he helps us to understand them. He urges parents to have a positive attitude and to form a strong attachment to their fussy baby. The rewards will come. As he says, "Babies who grow up in a nurturing environment with strong mother-infant attachment show enhanced intellectual and motor development."

Physicians learn a great deal during their years of schooling. However, they learn even more about human beings through their own life experiences. Dr. Sears is a pediatrician and father. This, plus his close association with the parents of his patients, has given him the knowledge and background needed to write this book. He profiles the fussy baby and explains why babies fuss. He also discusses fathering the fussy high-need baby, nighttime parenting, and parents' sexual feelings, their relationship with each other, and how having a fussy baby affects them and the rest of the family.

High-need babies often become high-need toddlers. Dr. Sears' approach to discipline and the development of trust and self-esteem can help parents through these trying times as well. Wrapping it all up is a wonderful descriptive case history of Jonathan. You will enjoy reading this story as you see yourself and your child through new eyes.

Parents are often asked if their baby is "good." Most people equate the "easy" baby with the "good" baby. But good means different things to different people. Sometimes being good means being wakeful and learning every minute, growing in every direction at once. Maybe your high-need child is on the way to being a genius or a leader in life, and you're helping now with your love, patience, and understanding

Betty Wagner Spandikow
Founder
La Leche League International

Preface

A fussy baby can bring out the best and the worst in a parent. This book is designed to bring out the best.

Early on in my pediatric practice I (Bill) realized that fussy babies are misunderstood. They are labeled difficult or demanding. Mothers would ask, "How long should I let my baby cry? Is it all right to pick him up every time he cries?" or "Is it all right to carry the baby all the time? Will I spoil him?" I was confused by these questions. The standard baby care advice suggested that parents "let the baby cry it out." But I was uncomfortable with this. It seemed unfair to both mother and baby. It was then I realized that because of their intense love for their babies, mothers are particularly vulnerable to advice about crying. But the advice was confusing them.

When we began to study the problem of why babies fuss, I started from the belief that babies do what they do because they are designed that way. Martha's intuition as a mother told her that there must be reasons for our babies' fussiness, and we agreed that mothers of fussy babies needed advice that did not go against their own intuition.

In this book we will share with you what we have learned from counseling several hundred parents of fussy babies. We will also share what we have learned from our personal experience of parenting a high-need daughter who has grown up to be a happy and successful young woman.

Throughout this book you will find practical tips on calming the fussy baby as well as personal testimonies from parents who have been there and survived. You will also find what you need to know to understand your fussy baby better. You will learn why babies fuss and what to do about it and why it is important to recognize your baby's unique temperament early in his life. We will also explore how the baby's temperament affects your parenting style and how your child's personality development is affected for better or worse by how you respond to his needs.

We hope that reading THE FUSSY BABY will enable parents to know their high-need child better and to help their child feel right. We hope it will also help both parents and children to enjoy each other more. These special babies require special parenting. High-need babies get used to a higher standard of living—and loving.

William Sears, MD
Martha Sears, RN

CHAPTER ONE

Profile of a Fussy Baby

"Uncontentable, that's what you are," sang a tired mother to her fussy baby as part of their late-afternoon crying and comforting ritual. This mother was able to vent her feelings through song and a bit of tired humor, and this got her and her baby through fussy times of the day.

Later, this same mother asked me, "Why is my baby like this? Other mothers don't spend hours and hours nursing and walking their babies. Am I doing something wrong?" Her questions are shared by thousands of new mothers who often feel overwhelmed by the incessant demands of fussy babies, but who are driven by uncompromising love to continue comforting and mothering their babies in need.

In the first days and weeks after birth, parents begin to understand the temperament of their baby. Some parents are blessed with so-called "easy" babies. Others are blessed with babies who are not so easy and who receive a variety of labels: exhausting baby, colicky baby, demanding baby, and fussy baby. The term "fussy baby" is a bit unfair. It implies that the baby's demands are excessive or unreasonable or perhaps the mother who describes her baby this way is unsympathetic or inept. Somehow, somewhere, someone is at fault. Instead of fussy baby, I prefer to call this special type of baby the "high-need baby." This is not only a more objective and kinder term, it also more accurately describes why these babies act the way they do and what kind of parenting they need.

Characteristics of High-Need Babies

High-need babies share certain traits. Every high-need baby may not show all of these behaviors all the time, and in my experience, many babies show some of these traits at some point during early infancy. Whether or not a baby is described as "high-need" depends on both the degree to which a baby exhibits these traits and the parents' perception of their baby's personality. Here are the ways parents have described their high-need babies to me.

"Supersensitive"

High-need babies are keenly aware of their environment. Noises and distractions cause them to startle easily during the day and make it difficult for them to settle at night. "Easily bothered" is how one mother described her sensitive baby. These children have short fuses and are easily disturbed by any changes which threaten the security of their environment. This sensitivity often affects their reactions to unfamiliar caregivers, and they show a high degree of anxiety about strangers. While parents may find this supersensitivity initially exhausting, later on it may be transformed from a liability to an asset. High-need children tend to be keenly aware of and curious about their environment.

"Intense"

High-need babies put a lot of energy into their behavior. They cry loudly, laugh with gusto, and are quick to protest if their "meals" are not served instantly. They seem to feel things more deeply and react more forcefully. "He's in high gear all the time," observed a tired father.

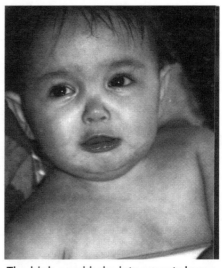

The high-need baby lets parents know what he needs.

High-need babies protest intensely when things are not to their liking. But they also are capable of forming strong attachments to their caregivers. A baby who strongly protests a separation from his parents is doing so because he is strongly attached to the parents. This close connection will help parents in the months and years to come, since it makes it possible for them to guide and influence their child's behavior.

"Demanding"

Mothers of high-need babies often sigh, "I just can't get to him fast enough." The baby conveys a real sense of urgency in his signals. "Red alerts" dominate his crying vocabulary. He has no respect for delays in gratification and does not readily accept alternatives if offered anything other than what he wants. If offered a rattle when he is expecting to be nursed, he will refuse to be distracted. His cries will intensify in protest at having been misread. Being demanding, however, is a positive and necessary character trait in high-need babies. It's what gets them the level of care they need to develop their full potential.

"I just can't put him down"

High-need babies crave physical contact. New parents may expect that babies will lie quietly in their cribs or sit passively gazing at adult activities or the latest in baby mobiles. This is certainly not the play profile of the high-need baby (or most other babies). These babies are not known for their ability to be alone. Mothers tell me, "He can't relax by himself." Mother's lap is his chair, her arms and chest his crib, her breasts are his pacifier. Inanimate mother substitutes are often forcefully rejected by these babies.

"He's always on the go"

"There is no such thing as a still shot," said one photographer-father of a high-need baby. "His motor seems stuck in fast idle," exclaimed another father. Constant motor activity goes along with the intense and supersensitive personality traits.

"Draining"

Parents inevitably confess, "He wears me out." A high-need baby uses up all of mother's and father's physical, mental, and emotional energy.

"Uncuddly"

While most babies melt and mold into the arms and over the shoulders of their caregivers, the high-need baby will often arch his back and stiffen his arms and legs, protesting any attempt to get him into a relaxed and cuddly position. The term hypertonic describes this muscular tightness. "I can feel the 'wirey' in him," one mother related. This tightness, combined with supersensitivity, makes some babies withdraw from close physical contact. They resist being hemmed in and are more comfortable being held at a distance or facing away from you. They are often the babies who hate being swaddled as newborns. They may want to be with a parent, but they also want to be in control of how closely they are held.

"Unsatisfied and unpredictable"

High-need babies are inconsistently appeased. What works one day often fails the next. As one exhausted mother exclaimed, "Just when I think I have the game won, the baby ups the ante."

"He wants to nurse all the time"

The term "feeding schedule" is not in the high-need baby's vocabulary. These babies often need prolonged periods of non-nutritive comfort sucking and are slow to wean.

High-need babies bring out the best in their parents.

"Awakens frequently"

These super-aware babies do not settle easily. They awaken frequently and seldom reward mothers with lengthy naps. "Why do high-need babies need more of everything but sleep?" lamented a tired mother.

The Outcome

Early in infancy, the character traits of high-need babies seem to be predominantly negative. But as the months progress, parents who are accepting of their baby's temperament and who respond to his needs gradually begin to see their baby in a different light. They use more positive descriptions, such as challenging, interesting, and bright. Those same qualities which at first seemed to be such an exhausting liability have a good chance of turning out to be assets for the child and the family later on. If the baby's cues have been picked up on and appropriately responded to in the early months, the intense baby may become a creative, sensitive, compassionate child. The little "taker" may later become a big giver.

Don't be too quick to predict what kind of person your child will become. Some difficult babies show a complete turnabout in personality later in childhood. But in general, the needs of these babies do not lessen; they only change.

What's in It for You?

One of the main themes of this book is that the temperament of the baby affects the temperament of the parents. In the following chapters, I shall discuss how a high-need baby can bring out the best in responsible parents.

CHAPTER TWO

Why Babies Fuss

"Why is my baby so fussy? Why can't I put her down?" asked a mother whose arms were worn out from constantly carrying her high-need baby. Not knowing why their baby is fussing is very frustrating for parents. In this chapter I want to give parents some information about why babies fuss and how baby and parents influence one another's behavior.

How a Baby's Temperament Is Formed

I use the term temperament to mean a baby's distinct, inborn natural disposition—the way her brain and body are wired to behave. Over time the child's reactions to the environment and the environment's influence upon the child interact to form the child's personality—the outward expression of her inner temperament.

Nature versus nurture

For centuries, philosophers and psychologists have debated the nature versus nurture question: whether it's primarily heredity or environment that determines how we become who we are. Today most behavioral scientists agree that a child is not a blank slate onto which caregivers can write a set of rules which will cause the child to act any way they wish. The child's inborn nature, which is determined largely by biology, has a great deal of influence on personality. At the same time, research has shown that the kind of care and stimulation a baby receives in the first year affects the developing brain. Appropriate stimulation and responsive care lead to the formation of better neurological pathways in the brain. Thus temperament, while important, certainly is modified by the caregiving environment, especially by the quality and quantity of mothering and fathering. One of the main premises of this book is that the caregiving environment can positively or negatively affect the temperament and personality of the high-need child.

Goodness of fit

The goodness of fit principle describes one of the most powerful influences on a child's temperament. The principle states that how a baby or child fits into her caregiving environment will affect the development of her personality either positively or negatively.

An infant comes wired with a temperament that is primarily genetically determined and is also influenced by the environment of the womb. While in the womb, the unborn baby fits perfectly into her environment—the temperature is constant and nutritional needs are automatically met. This is an environment of total fulfillment, generally free of any stress (although the mother's emotional state may have some effect on the infant). The baby doesn't have to do anything to get her needs met, and life in the womb is highly predictable.

Caregivers give a fussy baby what she needs to adjust to her post-birth environment.

Birth suddenly disrupts the picture. Baby's well-organized pre-birth life gives way to a whole new world. During the months following birth the baby tries to regain the sense of organization that brought her peace in the womb, but now she must *do* things in order to have her needs met. She is forced to act, to "behave." If hungry, she cries. She must make an effort to get what she needs from her caregiving environment. If her needs are simple and she can get what she wants without too much fussing, she is labeled an easy baby; if she does not adapt readily to what is expected, she cries and complains and ends up being labeled a difficult baby. Babies fuss when they are unhappy with the level of care they are being given, and fussy babies do not easily resign themselves to a lower level of care. When parents become more responsive, babies fuss less (Dihigo 1998).

The stimulus barrier

Why do fussy babies have more of a problem with fitting into the post-birth environment? One reason is that these infants have an immature stimulus barrier. This means that they don't block out disturbing stimuli as easily as other babies. For example, some babies will block out too much stimulation—the noise of the vaccuum cleaner, too many bright lights—by falling asleep. Many instinctively turn their heads away when they've had as much "conversation" as they can handle with an overeager auntie. These babies know how to keep themselves from getting overstimulated. Fussy babies are less able to block out disturbing stimuli. They are more aware of everything, and they fuss in order to alert others to their need for help in coping with all the excitement. They are appealing to their caregivers to act as a stimulus barrier for them and help them ignore disturbing sights and sounds in their environment.

Missing the womb

Another reason why babies fuss is what I call the "missing the womb" feeling. Being able to feel content is largely determined by the ability to adjust to change. The world of the unborn baby is a smooth continuum of experience in which she is lulled constantly by the sounds and movements of her mother and her needs are met consistently and automatically. Birth and the early weeks of adjustment to life outside the womb may cause fussy tendencies to surface. This new world doesn't feel like the womb, and it is a lot less predictable. The newborn wants to be comfortable, but doesn't know how to relax with all these strange new sensations. When she fusses, baby is saying, "I expect to feel good, but I don't, and I don't know what to do about it." She needs caregivers who will step in and give her what she needs to feel peaceful. They help her recover the comfortable feeling she enjoyed before birth. As caregivers do this, baby learns what makes her feel right. Eventually she will know how to help herself.

High need level

The need level concept provides another explanation for why

babies fuss. Some babies are more needy than others. Their mothers say, "She never seems satisfied." Fussy babies need a great deal of attention if they are going to feel comfortable, well-fed, and well-rested. Fortunately, babies who have high levels of need also come wired with an alarm system—their fussiness—that asks for a response from caregivers. Fussy babies are very demanding, but, believe it or not, this is a positive trait. If a baby were endowed with high-needs yet lacked the ability to communicate these needs, her survival would be threatened. Also, her emerging self-esteem would be in jeopardy because she would come to believe that she cannot get what she needs from others. I feel that high-need babies are inherently programmed to be demanding babies.

The most common example of demanding behavior in a high-need baby is the baby who "cries whenever I put her down." Before birth this baby had a sense of oneness with the mother. After birth the baby still does not feel like a separate individual. Baby continues to need a sense of oneness with mother. She needs to be close to mother's body, feel her movement, hear her voice, sense her breathing, and be enclosed in her arms. Try to put her down and she will protest. She doesn't know how to be peaceful on her own, so she needs and will demand continuing contact with mother. If this baby's needs are heard and filled, she will adjust more easily to her environment. She'll learn how to be on her own at her own pace, and she'll be a "better" baby.

What happens if a baby's demands go unheard and her needs unfilled? A need which is not filled doesn't just go away. Unfilled needs cause inner stress which sooner or later manifests itself as undesirable behavior, for example, anger, aggression, withdrawal, or rejection. This baby does not feel right on the inside and therefore, does not act right on the outside. A baby who does not act right is less of a joy to parent, and this causes baby and her unresponsive parents to drift further and further apart. The parent becomes less adept at giving, and the baby becomes less motivated to signal her needs. The entire parent-child relationship spirals downward.

The hurting baby

Some babies cry and fuss because they are in pain. I do not believe that this kind of discomfort should be dismissed as "just colic." this baby hurts, and her complaints should be investigated. Responsive parenting will help her cope with her discomfort while parents and pediatrician try to figure out what is bothering her. Chapter 5 explains more about the causes and cures for colic.

The Importance of a Responsive Caregiver

Babies with high need levels fuss primarily because of their own temperament, not because they're receiving poor mothering. Babies fuss because they must in order to fit. However, the responses they receive from their caregiving environment do play a part in determining whether or not babies with demanding temperaments acquire desirable or undesirable personality traits.

Consider the goodness of fit and need level concepts from the baby's viewpoint. A high-need baby who is trying desperately to fit into her environment may take one of two paths:

- She can fuss until she receives the level of care she needs.
- She can give up and resign herself to a lower standard of caregiving; withdrawal, apathy, and developmental delays—what I call the shut-down syndrome—may follow.

A high-need baby with a demanding temperament needs a responsive caregiver in order to feel in harmony with her world and to develop the positive side of her personality.

The world of the high-need baby revolves around a central attachment figure, a secure home base of operations. This role usually falls to the mother, though fathers and other adults the baby knows well can also be important attachment figures. (And if the mother of the high-need baby is going to survive and thrive, having back-up attachment figures is essential.) It takes two conditions for this trusting mother-infant bond to develop:

- The mother is available and increases her nurturing response to meet the needs of the baby.
- The baby shows attachment-promoting behaviors: smiling, sucking, cooing, clinging, gazing, and some form of protest when mother leaves. These behaviors make an infant irresistible to a parent.

A sensitive, responsive mother and a baby with good attachment-promoting behaviors are a good match, and a strong bond develops. When baby's behavior is fussy and disorganized, the mother's responsiveness becomes more important; she may need to increase her caregiving responses greatly in order to be rewarded with pleasant attachment-promoting behaviors from baby. When the baby does not show many attachment-promoting behaviors or the mother is unable to read and respond to the cues of the baby, a strong attachment may not develop.

Attachment means that mother and baby are in harmony. Baby gives a cue, and mother, because she is open to the baby's cues, responds. As baby learns that she will get a predictable and rewarding response, she is motivated to give more cues. As the mother and baby get to know and enjoy each other, the mother's responses become more spontaneous. Mother and baby become more sensitive to each other, and mother feels happier and more confident about meeting her baby's needs. She and the baby enjoy being together. As one mother put it, "I'm absolutely addicted to her."

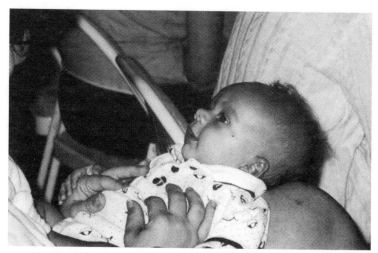

Developing a strong attachment with a high-need baby helps a mother to be more responsive.

Mothers with a strong attachment to their high-need babies sometimes say that the baby "seems glued to me." They also use the term "unglued" to describe their babies when they are protesting something in their environment. Nancy, a mother who worked long and hard to develop a strong attachment bond with her high-need baby, told me, "When the baby becomes unglued and seems to be falling apart, I now feel I can pick up the pieces and glue her back together. It has been a long tough struggle."

Mother as organizer

The mother plays a vital role in organizing her baby's behavior. Think of a baby's gestation period as lasting a full eighteen months—nine months inside the womb and at least nine more months outside. During the first nine months, mother's primary role is to nourish the baby and contribute to her physical development. The womb environment regulates baby's sensory and other systems automatically. Once outside the womb, baby continues to need assistance with regulating responses to stimuli, but now it's up to the mother and other caregivers to actively help the baby cope with her new environment. The more quickly a baby gets help with organizing these responses, the more easily she adapts to the puzzle of life outside the womb. The baby's attachment to the mother provides what she needs to begin to organize her behavior in all these ways:

- *Nutritional.* Mother provides nourishment with her milk.
- *Tactile.* Mother provides physical contact.
- *Visual.* Mother has a familiar face.
- *Auditory.* Baby grew accustomed to mother's voice and sounds prenatally.
- *Thermal.* Mother's body heat helps to stabilize the fluctuating body temperature of a tiny baby.
- *Vestibular.* Carrying and rocking help the baby develop her own sense of balance.
- *Kinesthetic.* Being held in mother's arms helps baby control her movements.
- *Olfactory.* A baby knows mother's familiar odor and the smell of her milk.
- *Sleep/wake patterns.* By sharing sleep with their babies, mothers help them organize their sleeping habits into a predictable day and night pattern.

By anticipating and filling her needs, mother helps baby adapt to a world where those needs are not automatically met. Without this responsiveness, the baby remains disorganized, and this results in fussy behavior. Fussing can be thought of as a withdrawal symptom, a result of the loss of the regulatory effects of attachment to the mother.

Tiny babies should not be left alone to learn to soothe themselves, as some parenting advisors would suggest. Tiny babies are not ready to function as separate individuals in the first months after birth. Experimental evidence supports this. When newborn animals are separated from the regulatory influence of the mother, they show "increased behavioral arousal" (Hofer

1978), in other words, fussy behavior. Babies who are nursed to sleep are less likely to become habitual thumb-suckers than babies who are left to soothe themselves to sleep (Ozturk and Ozturk 1977). Infants show more calm behavior when they're in touch with mother than when left alone (Brackbill 1971). Sleep disturbances are more common in babies who are separated from their parents at night (Sears 1985). Infants separated from their mothers show more unusual "self-rocking" behaviors (Hofer 1978). In my opinion, training babies to become self-soothers before they are ready and capable is as ridiculous as expecting a premature baby to provide her own medical care.

How the Temperament of the Infant Interacts with the Temperament of the Parent

A mother of a high-need baby once confided in me, "Our fussy baby absolutely brings out the best and the worst in me." This is certainly true. Just as babies come wired with different temperaments, mothers also have varying response levels. For some mothers, a nurturing response is automatic and is proportionate to the need level of their babies. For others, responses are not so automatic, and their nurturing abilities need to grow and mature. Understanding that a child's temperament affects the mother's nurturing ability is absolutely vital to the successful parenting of the high-need baby.

Easy baby/responsive mother

The so-called easy baby is a cuddly baby with good attachment-promoting skills whose needs are predictable and who just melts into the arms of anyone who holds her—the type of baby that everybody likes to be around. Because mothers tend to feel that the "goodness" of their babies reflects their effectiveness as mothers, the easy baby's mother feels that she is doing a good job at mothering and is delighted with the whole situation. An equally responsive mother who is struggling along with a more difficult baby may feel that she is not a very good mother.

"She Seemed Like Such an Easy Baby"

"Karen was such an easy baby. She never cried much. I could put her down for the night at 7:00 PM and she would sleep till morning. She seemed content with babysitters, which freed me up to do other things. But around four months, she started crying every time I put her down. She started awaking several times at night to nurse, and I finally had to sleep with her. She won't settle for any babysitter."

Dr. Sears comments: *Karen is what I call a delayed fusser. She finally got up enough nerve to demand what she needed. Crying and night-waking are normal attachment-promoting behaviors which help the baby develop by keeping mother close by. This baby was simply not going to settle for a lower standard of caregiving.*

Easy baby/less responsive mother

Because the easy baby is not very demanding, even a mother who by nature is less responsive may need to expend relatively little effort in developing creative comforting skills. This sounds like this is a good match between mother and baby, but the outcome is not always rosy. Because the easy baby seems so easily satisfied, the mother may expend relatively little energy on the baby and devote more attention to other more demanding activities and relationships, such as a more difficult child in the family or an outside job. She may feel that the baby "doesn't seem to need me that much." This may turn the baby into the "delayed fusser," a baby who starts out easygoing but who makes a complete turnabout in personality as time goes by. She becomes less content and eventually unleashes a burst of attachment-promoting skills (i.e., fussing and crying) with which she demands a higher level of response from her caregiving environment.

High-need baby/responsive mother

Another possible situation is the combination of a high-need baby who has good attachment-promoting behaviors with a responsive mother. In this situation, the mother cannot bear to ignore the incessant demands of the high-need baby. Her presence is always noticed. Her cries demand an instant response, which her parents are willing to provide. Once she has found her way into a comfortable spot in her mother or father's arms she refuses to be put down. Although this baby has high demands, the parents are rewarded by the feeling that their comforting measures are getting through to the baby and that they make a difference. The occasional satisfied response from the baby gives them the feeling that it is all worthwhile.

This type of demanding baby brings out the giving part of a mother's temperament. A high-need baby with good attachment-promoting skills matures the mother's nurturing response—as long as she remains open and responds to baby's needs without restraint. The mother must allow her intuitive nurturing to flow from her heart, uninhibited by the cultural norms of the neighborhood and unrestricted by conflicting advice from others. Even when the mother is confused about what baby needs, she experiments with alternate responses until she finds one that satisfies the infant. She becomes the baby's central attachment figure and develops the specific comforting skills that nurture her baby. Because the baby continually receives the nurturing response she anticipates, the baby refines her attachment-promoting skills. This in turn makes it easier for her caregivers to identify her needs and to comfort her. The entire parent-child relationship evolves into one of mutual sensitivity. The sensitive mother-infant pair enjoy each other more.

*"She Was
So
Uncuddly"*

"Rebekah was born into a family where mother, father, and two-year-old brother were all thrilled with her arrival. From the moment she was born, Rebekah showed little desire for cuddling. She would pull away from me after nursing and wriggle uncomfortably until I put her in her crib. She did not smile and avoided eye contact until she was nearly a year old. In spite of normal motor development, she indicated little interest in her surroundings. I shared my anguish and frustration with my pediatrician, but because she could find nothing physically wrong, she had no solution. I felt that somehow I had deprived this innocent child of something which was vitally needed—and yet I had no idea of what it could be. I really wanted to know her and to be close to her, yet there seemed to be an impenetrable wall between us.

"Shortly after Rebekah's first birthday, I became convinced that this behavior cycle needed to be broken. Very, very slowly we have seen some opening up in Rebekah. She has begun to share some of her feelings. With children her own age, she is becoming friendly and displays real leadership qualities. She still doesn't like to get too close, but on the whole, she seems to be better able to relate to her world and the people in it. She seems to need so much and yet is unable to receive."

Dr. Sears comments: *The uncuddly baby is the most difficult high-need baby to parent. These babies break the rules for promoting attachment. They do not smile,*

> *do not cry when they are put down, nor do they seem to take any pleasure in nursing. As a result, mother must initiate attachment behavior and work hard to maintain it even though the baby is giving neither cues nor appreciation. This baby does not automatically bring out the best in the mother. Instead, she requires the highest level of maternal giving in order to adjust to the world and communicate with others*

The high-need baby with poor attachment-promoting skills

These babies are often known as "non-cuddlers" or "slow to warm up." They withdraw and arch their backs when picked up to be held and fed. Non-cuddlers do not melt and mold to the contours of the parent's body when held in arms or over the shoulder and show little or no appreciation for parents' efforts to comfort them and communicate with them. Although I have found that most high-need babies do tell their caregiving environment what they need loudly and clearly, there are babies who do not demand the level of nurturing that they need. Because parents, especially mothers, are generally geared to wait for a baby's signals before responding, uncuddly babies do not bring out the best in mothers. In fact, studies have shown that mother-infant attachment is often less intense with non-cuddlers (Campbell 1979).

In order for a mother's nurturing responses to grow and mature, she must receive some appreciative feedback from the baby. Babies and children are not noted for verbally pouring out their gratitude to parents, but parents find that smiles, hugs, and other signs of positive emotion are very rewarding in themselves. If the mother does not receive this kind of feedback from her baby, there is a danger that the mother and baby will drift further and further apart. In this situation, interaction counseling really pays off. Mothers of non-cuddly babies who feel a bit shaky about their nurturing response ("I'm just not getting through") may do well to seek some counseling from professionals trained in mother-baby interaction. These are sensitive, experienced caregivers who can teach the mother how to recognize and respond to the more subtle cues of the non-cuddly baby. Mothers of uncuddly babies should beware of feeling that "the baby doesn't need me." This can deteriorate into feeling that "the baby doesn't like me." Uncuddly babies are often high-need babies in

A breastfeeding mother is programmed hormonally to respond to her baby's cries.

easy baby disguise. They need the best responses the parent can give in order for the best in themselves to develop.

The high-need baby and the restrained caregiver

A high-need baby and a restrained caregiver are at risk for problems. In this situation the baby may have intense attachment-promoting behaviors, but the mother sees these as negative behaviors that should not be reinforced. She tries to make a science out of child rearing, instead of letting herself go and following the nurturing instincts of her heart. Advice from well-meaning friends, relatives, and advisors sounds reasonable to her: "Let baby cry it out, you're making her too dependent." "You're picking her up so often, you're spoiling her." "She's manipulating you."

Mothers of high-need babies, beware of advice that suggests you restrain yourself from responding to your baby. If you are getting lots of this kind of advice, you are running around with the wrong crowd of advisors. This advice damages the mother-baby relationship because it encourages a new mother to follow rules rather than learn from her baby. Exhausted mothers of high-need babies are particularly vulnerable to any advice that others promise will work, but beware of quick and easy solutions that suggest adhering to rigidly scheduled feedings, bedtimes, and periods of crying—for example, "Let the baby cry forty-five minutes the first night, thirty minutes the second night, and she'll sleep through by the end of the week." This seldom works for any baby, but it is especially disastrous for the high-need baby.

Rigid schedules don't even make scientific sense. Humans are a continuous contact species; mothers and babies are made to stay close to one another. In some animal species, the mother can leave her young for extended periods of time to gather food. The mother's milk in these species has a high fat content which allows the baby animals to survive with widely spaced feedings. Human milk, on the other hand, is relatively dilute; it has a low fat and protein content which makes frequent, seemingly continuous feeding necessary. The mother is programmed for immediate nurturing responses. When she hears her baby's cries, the blood flow to her breasts increases, triggering her milk ejection reflex and reminding her to pick up and nurse the baby. A mother who falls prey to the advice to restrain her responses to her baby is going against her intuition and her biology. Following the dictates of outside advisors which run contrary to her heart is the first step toward making a mother insensitive to her baby, and insensitivity leads to mother-infant detachment. However, an unrestrained response to a baby's cries brings out the mother's nurturing qualities and builds trust between mother and baby.

What about the effect of restrained responses on the baby? A baby whose signals are not responded to may take one of two paths. She may increase her attachment-promoting signals, becoming more demanding, and cry until someone finally picks her up. Babies who take this approach may expend so much energy demanding the attention they need that they slow down developmentally. Studies have shown that infants are developmentally advanced in societies where attachment parenting and immediate nurturing responses are the rule rather than the exception (Geber 1958).

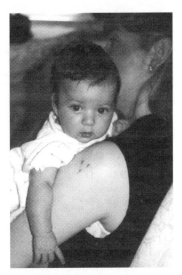

Nurturing responses to baby's cries enhance intelligence and temperament.

The other direction an infant may take when her signals are not responded to is to give up. Without a response, she is no longer motivated to communicate her needs, so she shuts down her signals and withdraws into herself, attempting to survive emotionally on a variety of ineffectual self-soothing habits. The baby attaches to objects rather than persons. In this situation both mother and baby lose. Neither has been able to profit from the skill of the other. The mother's nurturing responses have not been matured by the baby, and the disorganized nature of the baby's behavior has not been organized by the mother. The end result is a difficult relationship because of mutual insensitivity. The parent-child relationship may never recover from this difficult beginning.

Bringing Out the Best in Your Baby

The person your child becomes depends on inborn temperament and how it is nurtured. A variety of scales have been developed to evaluate the temperament and personality of infants. While these temperament tests help researchers compare the personalities of different babies, they are not especially helpful for parents, particularly those parents whose babies may be rated as "difficult." A difficult rating is not always a liability. For example, being "generally fussy on waking up and going to sleep" would be a temperamental characteristic that would earn the baby points as a difficult baby on most scales. Suppose the baby fussed because she didn't want to go to bed alone but was happy when she was allowed to fall asleep in her parents' arms and awaken in their bed; in my opinion, that's not an unreasonable demand. Another example: the baby who is able to soothe herself when upset gets a point for being easy while a baby who fusses until someone comes to comfort her is rated difficult.

Many of these parameters of infant temperament do not assess the baby at all. Instead they measure how closely the baby conforms to cultural expectations of what babies ought to be like, but really are not. People tend to think that easy babies are "better" babies, although the developers of these temperament tests do caution against this. A baby who fusses when put to sleep alone or fusses if no one picks her up has the strength of character to assert her personality and tell her caregivers what she needs. This baby is learning to be attached to persons rather than things. It would be more accurate to designate the "difficult" baby as an "assertive" baby or an "attached" baby. These are terms that are more descriptive and less value-laden. The term "difficult" makes a judgment which reflects the expectations of others rather than the baby's own temperament.

Nurturing your baby's personality

Nurturing responses to babies' cries enhance their temperament and intelligence. I believe that each child is endowed with a maximum intelligence potential which is primarily genetically determined. The child also comes wired with a set of behavioral traits that make up her temperament. These traits prompt caregivers to respond to the baby's needs. Predictable responses from caregivers make it easier for a child to learn that her signals have meaning and that she can make things happen. If a child can count on consistent feedback, the child becomes more

Getting Over Anger

"Steven, our two-year-old, and I just weren't getting along. After a lot of soul-searching, I discovered that my anger was hurting our relationship. I was angry with Steven for not being the baby I had expected and for wearing me out and not being as easy to handle as other babies. As soon as I recognized this anger and dealt with it, we both enjoyed each other more."

Dr. Sears comments: *In this situation, mother became angry because the baby she wanted was not the baby she got. Her anger toward her baby kept her from seeing her baby as an individual, a high-need baby who needed a high level of mothering. When she realized that her anger was keeping her from relating to her child, she began to see him for the unique person he was and stopped comparing him to other babies.*

adept at interaction. She is seen as more intelligent and more pleasant to be with.

A child with the potential for a high level of intelligence may also come wired with the temperament traits that merit her the label of demanding baby. She's smart, so she'll demand a high level of attachment and interaction with her environment. She'll want to be held all the time, to sleep with her mother, to nurse often. Being a demanding baby is beneficial to the child with a high intelligence potential, since interactions with caregivers are what's needed to make the most of her inborn intellectual ability.

Responsive caregiving is also important to a child's developing self-esteem. The smart baby who demands a high level of caregiving eventually learns to trust her environment. Because her parents trust her signals, she also learns to trust herself; in other words, she develops self-esteem. She gradually fusses less as her other communication skills develop. The child feels better about herself and therefore is able to interact more effectively with her environment. Her intelligence keeps right on developing as she learns to fuss less and communicate her needs in other ways.

What happens to the intelligence potential of a child whose cues are misread and whose assertive behavior is squelched—the baby who is left to cry it out? Ignore her cues and her intellectual development may suffer. This is like an artist who aspires to paint a special picture. If someone keeps taking away her brushes, either she'll never finish the painting (that is, reach her maximum potential) or she will accomplish the feat at a much slower rate and with a great deal of stress and frustration. There are many studies to support the correlation between intellectual development and a responsive caregiving environment. Babies who grow up in a nurturing environment with strong mother-infant attachment show enhanced intellectual and motor development.

Nobel prize winner Hans Selye, in his book *The Stress of Life*, proposes that stress can enhance intellectual development. How a person reacts to a stressful situation and resolves that stress can have a positive or negative effect on intelligence. Fussy babies seem to exude a lot of inner stress, but they are often not endowed with the ability to handle their own stress. This is why it is even more important for the intellectual growth of a fussy baby that she receive a nurturing response to stress. Resolving this stress may enhance her intellectual growth; unresolved stress may hinder it.

In this chapter I have presented an explanation of why babies fuss and how a baby's intelligence potential and temperament traits and the caregiver's responses all work together for the development of baby and parents. Subsequent chapters will explore practical ways to apply these ideas to parenting the high-need baby and child in order to bring out the best in parents and babies.

REFERENCES

Brackbill, Y. 1971. Effects of continuous stimulation on arousal levels in infants. *Child Dev* 42:17.

Campbell, S. B. 1979. Mother-infant interaction as a function of maternal ratings of temperament. *Child Psychiatr Hum Dev* 10:67.

Carey, W. B. 1994. The effectiveness of parent counseling in managing colic. *Pediatrics* 94:333.

Dihigo, S.K. 1998. New strategies for the treatment of colic: Modifying the parent/infant interaction. *J Pediatr Health Care* 12:256.

Geber, M. 1958. The psycho-motor development of African children in the first year and the influences of maternal behavior. *J Soc Psychol* 47:185.

Hofer, M. A. 1978. Hidden regulatory processes in early social relationships. In *Perspectives in Ethology,* ed. P. P. G. Bateson and P. H. Klopfer. New York: Plenum.

Lozoff, B. and Brittenham, G. 1979. Infant care: Cache or carry? *J Pediatr* 95:478.

Ozturk, M. and Ozturk, O. M. 1977. Thumbsucking and falling asleep. *Brit J Med Psychol* 50:95.

Sears, W. 1999. NIGHTTIME PARENTING. Schaumburg, IL: La Leche League International.

Selye, H. 1978. *The Stress of Life.* 2d ed. New York: McGraw Hill.

CHAPTER THREE

Right from the Start: Improving Your Baby's Temperament

Babies are born with unique temperaments, but the personalities they eventually develop are shaped by how parents respond to them. Certain characteristics of temperament, such as alertness, being demanding, wanting to be held all the time, ask a lot from adults. But these qualities may be needed to ensure that the child reaches his fullest potential. When parents respond to these challenging aspects of a baby's temperament, baby learns to channel these energies into positive behaviors. What parents do during the last months of pregnancy and the first two weeks after birth can have a dramatic and often lasting effect on the baby's temperament.

The Importance of a Peaceful Womb Environment

The unborn baby is aware of joys and stresses in his environment, and his temperament may be affected by his experience in the womb (Liley 1972; Verney 1981). This section is for parents who are expecting a baby and want to lower their risks of having a fussy baby, as well as for parents who already have a high-need child and would like to decrease the chances of the next baby being fussy. Parents can begin influencing their baby's behavior during pregnancy.

Most of the research on fetal awareness concerns babies' experiences during the last four months of pregnancy. The basic assumption underlying fetal research is that you can tell how an infant feels by the way he acts. You may be wondering how researchers can know how the fetus acts. Three noninvasive research tools have been used to study fetal emotions. The electroencephalogram (EEG) records changes in a baby's brain waves in response to environmental stimuli. Ultrasound, familiar to most pregnant women, uses sound waves to produce an image of the baby and his movement on a screen. Researchers also use fiberoptic techniques that allow them to actually see how the baby is reacting to outside stimuli.

There is not an exact correlation between a mother's emotional state during pregnancy and the temperament of her baby. A tense pregnant mother will not necessarily produce a tense baby. A peaceful womb environment is just one of many factors that influence babies' temperaments. What we are discussing in this section is just one way you may be able to lower your risk of having a fussy baby.

How the mother's emotional state affects her unborn baby

Mother and baby are part of the same hormonal network. Those same hormones that produce stress reactions in the mother (increased heart rate, increased blood pressure, flushing, sweating, headaches, etc.) pass through the placenta to the baby. So when mother feels upset, baby may be upset. Researchers theorize that an unborn baby who is continually exposed to high levels of stress hormones and who also produces his own stress hormones in response has a higher risk of developing an over-charged nervous system. As parents and others have said about fussy newborns, "It seems like he came wired that way." The following suggestions are aimed at creating pleasant communications between mother and unborn child.

Think the right thoughts. Research has shown that a mother's attitude toward her unborn baby may affect the baby's relationship with the mother later on. An old obstetric axiom states that if a mother rejects a fetus, that baby may later reject the mother. While certainly there is no clear-cut cause-and-effect explanation for this (nor is it true in all cases), research has shown that mothers experiencing unwanted pregnancies have a greater likelihood of having fussy babies, and they themselves have a lower tolerance for fussiness. This is certainly not a peaceful combination.

Sing the right songs. An expectant mother told me, "When my baby kicks and seems upset, I play music." Researchers in fetal awareness claim that babies, children, and even adults can recall songs that their parents sang to them *in utero*. Pregnant symphony musicians feel that music becomes a part of their babies before birth; some have noticed that music practiced by the mother during pregnancy is more easily learned by the child later on. Experienced mothers and fathers of fussy babies have related to me that the same lullabies and songs they sang before birth are the sounds that calm their babies after birth. These calming sounds were imprinted on the mind of the unborn baby, and he has learned to expect and respond to them. One of Pat Boone's daughters, Lori, shared with me how she, now herself a mother, still is calmed by the songs her daddy sang to her while in the womb.

Agitated unborn babies are calmed best by classical music (for example, Vivaldi, Mozart, music for flute and classical guitar), religious hymns, and folk songs. Fetuses have been shown to react violently to rock music. Dr. Thomas Verny, author of *The Secret Life of the Unborn Child* (1981), told of a mother who suffered a damaged rib at a rock concert because of her unborn child's strenuous kicks. Perhaps the violent display of fetal emotions was triggered by the aggressive rock music. Many mothers can tell when their fetus is upset and which of their own songs or other music has a calming effect. Unborn babies seem to have highly selective musical taste (which, as the father of teenagers, I have to report deteriorates as they get older). I advise mothers to keep a diary of those musical pieces that have a calming effect on their unborn babies so they can recall these tunes later during trying times.

Research has shown that a four- or five-month-old fetus hears and moves his body in synchrony to the rhythm of his mother's voice and songs. Just as pleasant sounds may soothe the infant, unpleasant, dissonant, and angry sounds may upset the unborn baby. The fetus has been shown to become agitated during times of parental fighting and will even move his hands over his ears when exposed to disturbing music.

Fathers, there is a part in this prenatal symphony for you, too. Studies have shown that when a father talked to his baby *in utero,* the baby was more responsive to his voice after birth. In my own practice, I have encouraged the prenatal custom of laying-on of hands. I encourage expectant couples to lay their hands on the uterus every night before going to bed, and talk, sing, and pray for the unborn child. Not only does this affirm their commitment to each other, it also soothes the baby. I believe the child inside senses that these two people who are joining hands over him will love and care for him. I advise fathers to take the lead in establishing this ritual, as this is a way of getting in touch and in tune with your baby before birth. Fathers who have enjoyed this custom throughout the final months of pregnancy have later confided in me, "Now I'm hooked. I can't get to sleep at night until I first lay my hands on the head of our newborn and reaffirm my commitment." Mother's and father's voices and songs seem to be like an acoustic umbilical "chord" which is not severed at birth but unites parents and child for a long time thereafter.

Dance the right dance. When your unborn baby

Fathers can communicate with their baby before birth.

seems agitated, experiment with various gentle movements until you find one that calms the baby. You may need to call upon this same dance step later on. One mother related to me that rhythmic swimming would settle her unborn baby.

Feel good feelings. How a mother feels about herself during pregnancy may have a bearing on how the fetus feels about himself. Researchers in fetal awareness believe that fetuses are most affected by chronic and unresolved stress in the mother. The fetus is much less agitated and less likely to be permanently affected by normal life stresses that are quickly recognized and quickly dealt with. Studies have also shown that a mother's attitude toward pregnancy can become a self-fulfilling prophecy (Verney 1981). Mothers who were fearful of childbirth and expected a difficult labor were more likely to have a traumatic birth; the infants of these mothers were more likely to be fussy babies. Women who were ambivalent about becoming a mother were more likely to have apathetic babies; it was as if the fetus picked up these mixed messages and came into the world confused and untrusting of his caregivers. Mothers who were downright rejecting of their fetus throughout their pregnancy were the group most likely to have emotionally disturbed infants. The mothers in this study who had pregnancies that were relatively trouble-free emotionally were the most likely to be in harmony with their babies after birth. In these fetal outcome studies, the single most important contributing factor to a mother's emotional well-being during pregnancy was the involvement of a loving and caring husband. Fathers do indeed play a vital role in nourishing the temperament of their unborn children.

The womb environment establishes a child's expectations of the world to come. If the womb has been predominantly a harmonic and loving environment, the child is likely to expect the same from the world he enters, possibly predisposing him toward a cuddly, trusting, calm temperament. If the womb has been hostile because of the mother's emotional state or her use of drugs or alcohol, the baby may enter his world distrustful and fussy and may not easily fit into his environment. This newborn's parents may describe their baby by saying, "He came out fighting."

A word of caution. Please bear in mind that no one's life is stress-free, especially during all the changes of pregnancy. The normal ups and downs of prenatal emotions will not do babies harm. In fact, understanding and coping with these feelings is part of a woman's preparation for motherhood. What a woman is feeling during pregnancy is not nearly so important as what she does about it. If you are dealing with constant marital stress or negative feelings about your pregnancy, get some professional help before your baby is born. Finding ways to live with and resolve the stress of a complicated life may improve your baby's womb environment, and it certainly will make you better prepared to cope with the stress of parenting.

Attachment Parenting

How a mother and baby get started with each other can have a profound impact on achieving two important parenting goals: smoothing out the temperament of the baby and building up the sensitivity of the mother. In this section I will present a parenting style which will help you get to know your baby better and respond to his needs in the early weeks of life. You'll learn more about this parenting style, called attachment parenting, in the chapters that follow. Attachment parenting will help both you and your child grow and flourish during the first year and the years to come.

The suggestions that follow in this section are all geared toward helping parents get connected to their baby. Connected means not only that you care for and care about your baby, but also that you can understand your baby, imagine what he's feeling, and know what to do about it. Attachment parenting, with its emphasis on keeping parents and baby close, gives you and your baby lots of practice at communicating with one another. Staying close calms baby, develops parents' intuition, and helps everyone in the family get along because they know and trust one another.

Prenatal preparation

Take a childbirth class to prepare for your baby's birth. Learning about birth will help you and your baby enjoy a smooth transition from pregnancy to parenting. You need to know about how your body gives birth naturally and how you can minimize your own fears and tensions and work with your body. A birth that allows you and your baby the most natural passage possible, with minimal interventions, will help the two of you get off to a good start. Talk to your doctor about the kind of birth you want. Educate yourself so that you can be an active member of the health care team. You will have more confidence in yourself as a parent if you get involved in your baby's care even before he is born.

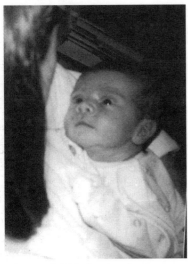

A peaceful birth experience enhances attachment behaviors.

The prenatal period is a good time to read as much as you can about infant development and get involved with some parent support groups. In my opinion, the support group that best prepares a mother to handle a fussy baby is La Leche League, the organization that provides new mothers with information about breastfeeding. At monthly LLL meetings, mothers learn about breastfeeding and also about responsive mothering. LLL Leaders are available by phone to answer questions about breastfeeding and mothering infants. The mother-to-mother support available from La Leche League is a lifeline for many new mothers struggling to adjust to a fussy baby and a new way of life.

The prenatal period is also a time to strengthen your marriage bond and for parents to reaffirm their commitment to each other. A stable and fulfilled marriage is absolutely necessary for successful parenting of a fussy baby.

A peaceful birthing experience

There is a saying in pediatrics that an anxious birth may produce an anxious baby. Studies have shown that babies who are the product of a birth characterized by fear and pain and who are separated from their mothers in the hours after birth are more likely to become fussy babies. There is also a higher incidence of fussy and colicky babies among mothers who have been heavily medicated during childbirth (Meares 1982). Medications used during childbirth may affect infant behavior during the entire first month of life (Sepkosi 1992) and can

*Off to a
Bad Start*

"When we went home on the fifth day after my cesarean, Michael seemed to settle right into a four-hour feeding cycle—until about 8:00 PM on the first evening. The infamous fussy baby hour had begun, and so had night after night and day after day of no sleep. I was insecure about being a mother. I did not grow up around babies and knew nothing about taking care of them. I didn't know what to expect. In spite of all the advice and warnings to the contrary, the thing I focused on was that my girlfriend's baby who was two months older than Michael had slept through the night ever since he was born.

"Needless to say, by the second day home I was angry and frustrated, and by day three I was wondering why I had ever wanted a baby. The incessant nursing really drove me out of my mind. Michael would nurse for the longest time but would be satisfied for such a short time. I wanted to do the best thing for my baby, but I dreamed of bottles, particularly at night.

"Everyone told me new mothers should sleep when the baby sleeps, but I could not fall asleep during the day. In fact, I couldn't even relax. I expected to hear Michael cry at any given second.

"No other mother in my entire family had ever breast-fed successfully. They told me, 'He must be hungry. Babies just don't cry all the time.' Besides this defeatist attitude about breastfeeding, I knew that Michael's

constant need for attention was driving them crazy.
This was not a baby who ate and went to sleep. This
baby ate, dozed, ate, and cried, cried, cried. He never
seemed to be satisfied.

"Finding out from Dr. Sears that this was simply (!)
the high-need baby syndrome was somewhat of a
relief, but when I got home and sat down in my rock-
er to nurse Michael, I began to cry. I felt that I could
not cope with a baby like Michael. That sense of
despair has only gradually diminished.

"At about two-and-a-half months Michael began
responding and doing all the things that make having
a baby fun. At about eight months he started sleeping
fairly consistently. Despite the inconvenience and hor-
rible feelings I went through, I was glad I persisted
because I now have one of the happiest and most
secure babies that I know."

make it more difficult for a baby to learn to breastfeed effectively (Walker 1997). A peaceful birthing experience followed by
time for mother and baby to be together helps to get breastfeeding off to a good start.

Of course, you cannot control everything that happens during birth. There will be situations where medical intervention is
necessary for the health of mother and baby. With some mothers and babies, technology plays an important role during labor
and delivery. While this may increase your chances of having a
fussy baby, remember that birth is only the beginning. You have
many hours, days, and weeks ahead of you in which to mother
your baby.

Bonding and rooming-in

Unless medical complications make it impossible, arrange to keep your baby with you from birth on. This eases your baby's transition from the womb to the outside world. Having your baby room-in with you while you're in the hospital helps to smooth his temperament and builds up your sensitivity. Right from the start you can teach your baby to trust you to meet his needs promptly.

Respond promptly to your baby's cries

Promptly responding to baby's cries develops your sensitivity to his unique language. It also teaches the fussy baby to cry more effectively. Chapter 4 explains more about why babies cry and what to do about it.

Breastfeed your baby

Unrestricted breastfeeding helps a mother to become more sensitive to her baby's cues. It also helps baby develop better communication skills because mother responds to his fussiness with a predictable nurturing response—nursing. Allowing the baby to wean himself helps develop his internal feeling of rightness. See Chapter 7 for more information about the advantages of breastfeeding for fussy babies.

Nighttime parenting

Fussy babies tend to awaken easily because they carry their sensitive temperaments into their sleep patterns. Welcoming your baby into your bed (the concept of sharing sleep) helps baby organize his sleep patterns and awaken less. Chapter 9 provides tips on parenting fussy babies through the night.

Father involvement

Mothers who have coped well with a high-need baby often tell me, "I could not have survived without the support of my husband." High-need babies and their mothers need active involvement from fathers. The special challenges that high-need babies present for fathers are detailed in Chapter 8.

Close contact

Keep your baby with you. This strengthens your commitment to parenting and enhances your sensitivity to your baby and to each other. "Wearing" a fussy baby in a baby sling or carrier helps to mellow baby's mood and makes fussing less necessary. Baby-wearing works for fathers as well as mothers. For more about soothing your baby by keeping in close contact, see Chpater 6.

Attachment Parenting: What's in It for You?

In my many years of pediatric practice, I have observed how some parents of high-need babies build up their sensitivity more than others. The most sensitive parents are usually the ones who have used attachment parenting to meet their baby's needs.

Builds up your sensitivity

The attachment style of parenting begins with a spirit of openness, being open to the cues of your child and being open to the intuition of your heart. Openness to your child is the first step in becoming a sensitive parent. The more you are open and responsive to your baby's demands, the more sensitive you become and the easier it is for you to know what your baby needs. The attachment style of parenting helps mother and baby be in harmony with each other. Starting off this parent-child relationship in harmony is the best way to mellow the temperament of the fussy baby.

Makes you more intuitive

Every baby comes wired with a unique level of need, based upon his individual temperament and ability to adjust to his

> ## "Other Mothers Seem to Have More Control"
>
> "Why can't I handle my baby? I can't get him to stop crying or go to sleep or get on a schedule. I can't put him down and leave him like other mothers can. Other mothers seem more in control of their babies than I am. Why are other mothers better at this?"
>
> **Dr. Sears comments:** *Don't compare your baby with other babies. How easy the baby is to handle does not reflect your effectiveness as a mother. Your baby fusses as much as he does primarily because of his own temperament, not because of your mothering abilities. Mothers tend to exaggerate the "goodness" of their babies, and you may be seeing these other mothers' babies only at their good times. Remember the parent-child law of supply and demand: your baby demands so much because he needs so much. His demands are geared to bring out the best in his caregivers so that his temperament can develop in the right direction.*

caregiving environment. Every baby is also endowed with an instinctual ability to give cues to his caregivers, telling them what he needs. Babies with higher needs give stronger cues. For example, a baby who needs to be held all the time cries when his caregiver attempts to put him down. Most babies have no problem giving cues, but recognizing these cues and responding to them is the big challenge in parenting the high-need baby.

Every parent also has the ability to interpret the baby's cues and a sort of radar system that stays tuned into the baby. This is often called mother's (or father's) intuition. When the need level of the baby and the intuitive abilities of the parent match, the pair is in harmony. Baby fusses less and parents feel confident. When the needs and cues of the baby baffle the intuition of the parents, the family struggles. Years of observing parents and babies have led me to conclude that a law of parenting economics governs each parent-child relationship—the law of supply and demand. Parents *will* be able to meet the needs of their individual child, providing they adopt a parenting style that allows them to be more sensitive to their baby's demands.

Occasionally a mother will share with me, "Sometimes I don't feel like I have any intuition. I just don't know what my baby needs." One of the main purposes of this book is to help parents build up their sensitivity to their baby—their intuition. Intuition is really nothing more than an accumulation of experience that makes it possible for you to understand and respond to your baby without a lot of thinking. If you put into practice the features of attachment parenting listed above you will learn to respond intuitively to your baby.

Increases your mothering hormones

The attachment style of parenting builds a "hormoneous" as well as a harmonious relationship. Unrestricted breastfeeding raises mother's prolactin levels. This hormone, which regulates the production of milk, may also help mothers cope with the stress of mothering a new baby. I like to think of prolactin as a "perseverance hormone" that gives mothers an extra boost during trying times. Oxytocin, the hormone that triggers a breastfeeding mother's milk ejection reflex, also brings a sense of calm and may help a mother be more loving toward her baby. On the surface it may look as if the attachment style of parenting is all giving, giving, giving, but bear in mind that when mothers are open and giving to their babies, the babies give something back by stimulating these natural stress-busting hormones. When you let the mother-baby relationship operate the way it was designed to, there is mutual giving.

May prevent fussiness

Studies show that babies who are held a great deal and whose parents respond promptly to their cries learn to cry less. You will read more about this in the next chapter. Practicing attachment parenting right from the start may keep a potentially fussy baby from becoming one or may lessen the degree of his fussing. Many babies will start out as easy babies, but around two weeks of age (after what I call the "grace period")

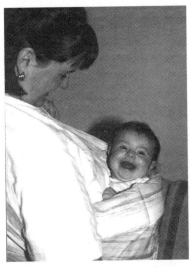

Babies who are held more learn to cry less.

they "wake up" and become difficult. Mothers will often relate, "He was such an easy baby the first couple of weeks, but now he's a different person." I feel that some of this delayed fussing could be prevented by giving the babies greater harmony in their environment right from the start, before they have to fuss to ask for it. Babies who do not receive responsive parenting right from the start may begin to protest to tell their caregivers that change is in order.

What's in It for Your Child?

At this point parents may be wondering, "Does parenting style really make any difference? Can I really have that much of an effect on my baby's personality?" The answer is a resounding yes! Certainly parents should not take all the blame or all the credit for the way their infant turns out, but studies have shown that parenting styles do make a difference.

Babies feel better

A baby who is the product of the attachment style of parenting feels right. A baby who feels right acts right. These babies don't have to begin fussing to get what they need or at least they don't have to fuss for long. This internal feeling of rightness mellows the internal stress and disorganization that characterize many fussy babies.

Babies grow better

Besides behaving better, babies parented with the attachment style show better physical and intellectual development. Babies who have a strong mother-infant attachment use the mother to get their needs met and to help them calm down in times of stress. As a result, these babies don't waste energy spinning their wheels with ineffectual self-comforting measures. Instead, they use their energy for growth and development.

Discipline is easier

Attachment parenting's big pay-off comes as children grow. The trusting, responsive relationship you start to build in infancy becomes the basis of the way you guide and discipline your child in the years to come. Everything that follows is easier if you learn to know and respond to your child right from the start.

REFERENCES

Liley, A. 1972. The fetus as a personality. *Aust NZ J Psychiatr* 6,99.

Meares, R. et al. 1982. Some origins of the 'difficult' child. *Brit J Med Psychol* 55:77.

Sepkoski, C. M. et al. 1992. The effects of maternal epidural anesthesia on neonatal behavior during the first month. *Dev Med Child Neurol* 34:1072.

Verney, T. 1981. *The Secret Life of the Unborn Child.* New York: Dell.

Walker, M. 1997. Do labor medications affect breastfeeding? *J Hum Lact* 13:131.

CHAPTER FOUR

Crying Guide for New Mothers

"If only my baby could talk, I would be able to know what she wants," exclaimed a new mother. "Your baby can talk," I replied. "You need to learn how to listen." This chapter is about interpreting your baby's crying. It will help you:

- Understand why babies cry
- Improve your listening skills
- Increase your sensitivity
- Teach your baby to cry "better"
- Lessen your baby's need to cry.

When I first wrote this chapter, I sent out several hundred questionnaires asking parents about commonly given baby advice. One of the questions was, "What advice do you get about responding when your baby wakes up crying or cries to be held all the time, or when she cries if you put him down?" The most common advice parents received was:

"Let her cry it out."
"She's got to learn to be independent."
"She's manipulating you."
"Crying is good for her lungs."

Another part of my questionnaire asked parents how this advice made them feel. The most frequent responses were:

"I can't do it."
"It goes against my instinct."
"It doesn't feel right to me."
"I can't let her cry when I know I have the means
  to comfort her."

Ninety-five percent of mothers responded that the advice to let their babies cry didn't feel right to them. I have learned to place great value on mothers' gut feelings—ninety-five percent of mothers can't be wrong. This questionnaire also showed me that there is an incredible conflict between mothers' own intuition and what other people are telling them.

Things have not changed much in the seventeen years since this book was originally published. Every few years another so-called "baby expert" writes a book telling parents it's okay not to respond to their babies' cries. In fact, these advisors promise that your child will be better off in the long run if you let her "cry it out" alone in a crib. Mothers still tell me that this advice feels wrong to them, and my years of researching and writing books about attachment parenting have not turned up any evidence to support the idea that crying is good for babies.

Because of this continuing confusion about how to respond to infant crying, this chapter is the longest and most detailed in the entire book—as it was when the book was first written. It is important because your understanding of your baby's cry and what to do about it will influence many other aspects of your

Responding is a good way to learn why your baby is crying.

parenting. The relationship you build with your baby today is the foundation of how the two of you will communicate in all the years to come.

It has always upset me as a pediatrician that babies' cries are so poorly understood by adults. I feel like an attorney pleading the case for my little client who does not yet have the language skills to stand up before her caregivers (and the people who advise them) and say, "Please hear me out."

Why Babies Cry

In the first few months of a baby's life, there is a real paradox: a baby's needs are great but her ability to communicate these needs is limited. A baby cannot tell us in plain language what she needs. But while a baby is unable to communicate clearly in the first months of life, the baby does have a way to let caregivers know that she needs attention. It's a language called crying.

If a baby doesn't cry, both the baby and the parent are in trouble. Although the meaning of a cry is not always plain, you can be sure that when a baby cries, she is trying to communicate that she needs something. Offering to help is a mother's natural response—and responding is a good way to start learning about why your baby is crying.

> But what am I?
> An infant crying in the night,
> An infant crying for the light,
> And with no language but a cry.
> —*Alfred Lord Tennyson*

How does the cry work? The infant first senses a need or, at least, the "not right" feeling that accompanies a need. The realization of this reflexively triggers the sudden inspiration of air followed by forceful expiration. The forcefully expelled air passes the tightened vocal cords, and the vibrating cords produce a sound we call a cry. Different babies sound different, and mothers can distinguish between their baby's cries and those of other babies a matter of hours after birth. Researchers call these unique sounds cry prints. These are similar to voice prints which are as unique to each individual as fingerprints.

Crying is about more than sound. It also involves body language. To be fully appreciated, the baby's cry needs to be seen as well as heard. In fact, studies have shown that even experienced mothers cannot always decode the meaning of their babies' cries if they cannot see the baby. The baby's face reflects the intensity of the cry. In a cry of mild distress, a baby's eyes are open and only the area around the mouth is contorted. As the crying intensifies, the signs of distress travel up the baby's face: closed eyes, wrinkled eyebrows, and furrowed forehead. Your baby's facial expression will give you clues about what she needs.

A Crying Glossary

Cries are triggered by needs, and babies will produce different signals depending on what they need and how badly they need it. Here's what different kinds of cries look and sound like. (Don't spend too much time trying to de-code the baby's cry. The best way to figure out why baby is crying is to respond quickly.)

Cries of pain

Pain cries begin suddenly, reach a high pitch quickly, and then seem to stay at that shrill pitch for an eternity. Toward the end of the first breath of the cry, the pitch tapers off as the baby begins to run out of breath. The sound as baby takes her next breath is harsh, almost croupy, as she quickly builds up a new supply of air power for the next yell. The initial piercing sound of the pain cry as well as the look on baby's face goes right to the heart of anyone within earshot. Baby's mouth is wide open as if to say "ouch." The baby's furled tongue and open jaws quiver; her fists are clenched, legs drawn up. The part of the pain cry that really gets to me is toward the end of the breath when baby's quivering lips begin to turn blue and just for a moment no sound is produced; finally, the baby takes her next breath.

Cries of hunger

Hunger cries begin less suddenly than pain cries and build up more gradually. They are shorter and less shrieking and have a sustained high frequency and a rising and falling melody. The hunger cry contains frequent pauses, as if giving mother at least a few seconds to get her blouse up before the baby starts another round of more intense signals. Before the cry starts, there are other telltale clues of hunger–restlessness, mouthing the fingers, nuzzling at the breast–that give the mother a chance to respond even before a cry is necessary.

Cries of anger

Anger cries are sustained cries with a pronounced vibrato. They are pitched lower than pain or hunger cries. The hoarse sounds throughout cries of anger are caused by the turbulence of excess air being forced through the vocal cords. Sometimes there is a bubbly sound to the cry as the air vibrates the saliva in baby's throat. The lips are often a clue to the anger cry. They are tightly clenched, pursed. Hunger cries that are ignored can become angry cries.

Cries of illness

The cries of an infant who just isn't feeling well tend to be of lower pitch and intensity. The weepy, whiney "uh-uh" sound calls forth sympathy from the caregiver rather than an immediate red-alert response.

"I want attention" cries

Bored cries are whiney, low-pitched murmuring sounds that get noticed but do not set off an internal alarm in the listener. Most parents easily decode baby's "pick me up and do something with me" cries.

Tired cries

When a baby is crying because she's tired, the cries are longer in duration and have a noticeable vibrato and a wailing siren-like sound.

Crying Signals and Parents' Responses

Infant cries have several unique features. First, the cries of early infancy are of reflex origin; they are automatic. A tiny infant does not have to stop and think, "Now, what kind of cry will get my dinner served?" This initial reflexive crying is later refined into more purposeful and deliberate communication as the infant's language skills develop. Second, the signal is easily generated; the infant initiates crying with very little effort. Third, the cry is disturbing enough to alert the caregiver to attend to the baby and stop the cry. Scientists have found that the infant cry is one of the loudest of all human sounds, ranging from eighty to eighty-five decibels—equivalent to the noise of an unmuffled truck. Fourth, the cry is usually not so disturbing as to make the caregiver avoid contact with the baby. The cry vanishes when the need for it is past. You may not have thought of it this way before, but all of these features make the infant cry a perfect signaling system.

The fact that an infant cry is a signal is important to

An infant cry is a signal intended to influence a caregiver to respond.

remember. A signal is more than just a sound. It has meaning. It is intended to influence the behavior of another. An infant cry is a signal that helps the baby get the things she needs to survive. It activates parents' emotions and stirs them into action. Using the term "activate" implies that something on the receiving end of the signal is tuned in to the right frequency, ready to respond. I believe this is true. Adults and even children want to do something to help in response to infant cries. Studies have shown that women in general respond to an infant's cries more intuitively and with less restraint than do men, and a breast-feeding mother responds to her own infant's cries with measurable changes in her body chemistry. Certain hormones are released, and there is an increase in blood flow to her breasts (Vuorenkoski 1969). She may experience a milk ejection reflex accompanied by the urge to pick the baby up and nurse and comfort her. Fathers find it easier to "let the baby cry" because they do not have such an unmistakable biological response to a baby's cries.

A sensitive mother told me once how guilty she felt when her husband discovered their two-day-old baby crying in their bedroom. He carried the baby, still upset and crying, into the family room, and when the mother saw her squalling newborn, she was instantly overwhelmed with guilt. Up until then the baby had been kept near her, within hearing and seeing distance. This time she had not been available to recognize the baby's early distress signals, and the baby's body language made it obvious that she had been crying for several minutes already. The mother recalled this episode vividly two years after the event took place.

Even little children have built-in responses to babies' cries. One day a mother brought her two-year-old daughter and her one-month-old baby into the office for an exam. When the baby began to cry, the two-year-old quickly ran to her mother, pulled on her skirt, and exclaimed, "Mommy, baby cry. Pick up." The mother then said, "She's always like that. I can't get to her baby sister fast enough." When our daughter Hayden was six years old, we loved to watch her immediate nurturing response to the cries of her two-year-old sister, Erin. We called this the "zoom" response. Whenever Erin would wake from her nap with a cry, Hayden was off like a flash, breaking all speed records to go and comfort her little sister.

Beginning with the first meeting with your newborn, think of your baby's cry as a signal to be valued, not a habit to be broken. This starts your crying communication network off on the right "note." Your baby's cries are a language to be listened to, fine-tuned, and responded to.

How much does the "usual" baby cry?

Most studies of crying babies show that babies begin to cry more often around two weeks of age. The amount of crying peaks around six to eight weeks and then markedly subsides around the fourth to sixth month.

Many studies state that infants cry "an average of two to

three hours each day." I urge parents to beware of drawing any conclusions from these studies of crying. These studies, which are widely quoted in books for parents, might lead one to think that it is normal, even okay, for babies to cry two to three hours a day. I do not personally believe this. In my own practice and personal experience I would certainly not consider it normal for babies to cry two to three hours a day, and I don't want parents to conclude that it is all right to let their babies cry two to three hours a day. The mothers in these studies were not given any counseling about what to do when their babies cried and were not specifically advised to use their mothering skills to minimize their babies' crying. In studies where researchers or experienced mothers teach new mothers how to interpret and respond to their babies' needs, the amount of time babies spend crying is dramatically reduced. (Dihigo 1998; Wolke 1994). When you recognize that a cry is a signal and you respond appropriately, the crying should diminish and end. In cultures in which an immediate nurturing response is the normal response to an infant cry, the amount of daily crying is reported in terms of minutes, not hours.

But how do I respond?

When your baby cries, act! Don't think, just respond. Follow that first little blip that appears on your radar screen. This is your intuition. It may not be able to tell you exactly what's wrong, but it does tell you that your baby needs your assistance or support. Follow your feelings and act immediately and without restraint. Here's why.

Babies who receive an immediate nurturing response to their cries eventually cry less frequently and with less intensity. When they do cry, their cries are less disturbing. Immediate nurturing responses teach babies to cry "better."

What do I mean by cry "better"? There is an important difference between mechanical signals, such as those on a train or an automobile, and a baby's crying signals. Babies modify their signals based on the responses they get. The other part of the signaling network—the mother—provides feedback on the signal quality. Mothers' responses are what teach babies that their signals have meaning. Respond often enough and baby learns to expect a nurturing response. She learns that she can make things happen in her world, and she learns to trust that some predictable person will come and help her cope with her feelings of distress. As baby learns these lessons, she discovers that she doesn't have to cry hard and desperately to get what she needs. In fact, she may be able to communicate what she needs with a less intense sound, or even a look or a gesture. She learns that she can count on her parents for food and comfort. She gets used to feeling right and eventually learns to feel right much of the time, with less and less assistance from caregivers.

It may take longer for a fussy baby to settle into feeling calm much of the time. As her needs for comfort decline, other needs will take their place—for example, the need to be kept safe as she enthusiastically explores her environment. She will still require lots of attention. But an early investment in answering the signals of a high-need baby will pay off in a more trusting relationship and better communication that will make your job as a parent easier in the months and years to come.

What's Wrong with "Crying It Out"?

Let me prepare you for an objection that some people may throw at you when you insist on picking up your baby every time she cries. They will tell you picking your baby up every time she gives a signal reinforces manipulative behavior and puts the baby rather than the parent in charge.

As a self-appointed activist in the "Stamp Out Restrained Parenting Movement" (one who has more than two decades of experience), let me offer a logical defense against these objections: parents who quickly respond to a baby's pre-cry signals are actually reinforcing these more peaceful ways of communicating. By being sensitive to the pre-cry signals, you are rein-forcing the development of other types of communication and body language (for example, squirming, nuzzling, vocalizing, and reaching). As your baby becomes more verbal and more capable of soothing herself, you will find that your response time can comfortably lengthen. When you do not respond to the opening signals, you teach your baby that all-out crying is the best way to get quick results. This is much more likely to "spoil" the baby.

Unwarranted fears of "manipulative" babies continue to characterize the parenting styles of contemporary mothers and fathers. New parents are confronted with a flurry of confusing advice concerning responses to babies' cries. Even though child development researchers have demonstrated the importance of responsive parenting, misguided childcare writers (many with dubious credentials) still attempt to tell parents how to control the normal sounds of babies and how to train them to keep quiet and quickly achieve independence. In my opinion, they have succeeded only in producing individuals who are likely to grow up to be selfish and preoccupied with their own needs. They have not learned the important lesson that human beings at their best are interdependent—they need one another in order for each one to achieve his or her full potential.

The case against "crying it out"

Should babies be left to cry? No! When someone gives you the "let the baby cry it out" advice, ask what he or she means. You'll probably receive an answer something like this: "She's only cry-ing out of habit. She knows crying will get her what she wants and she wants to manipulate you." Then ask, "How do you know she's not crying because of a real need?" As the dialogue goes on, your advisor should become increasingly aware of how unfair it is for someone to judge the language of a tiny baby without having all the facts, especially someone who has no bio-logical attachment to that baby.

Why is the "cry it out" advice so common? Understanding the thinking behind this advice will help you understand how it became so widespread.

Rigid, restrained parenting. The "let your baby cry" advice comes from a parenting philosophy that preaches restraint. It comes with an unwarranted fear of babies "manipulating" vulnerable parents, who, as adults, are supposed to be the ones in control. Parents are led to expect quick and easy methods for controlling their children. The "let the baby cry it out" advice fits in nicely with the rest of the program, which also includes rigid schedules, breastfeeding by the clock, and doing everything by the book.

Busy, inexperienced parents want quick answers to their baby-rearing dilemmas. Rigid methods of parenting promise quick results. A good example is the classic dictum, "Let your baby cry. She will cry for forty-five minutes the first night, only thirty minutes the second night, and by the end of the week she'll learn to sleep through the night, and there's the end of your problem." Parents, remember that difficult problems in child care do not have easy answers.

Spoiling. "But you'll spoil the baby by picking her up every time she cries." This is another reason given to justify the "let your baby cry it out" advice. Spoiling is an unfortunate idea that crept into child-care language and got a firm hold in discipline concepts before anyone really analyzed what the word meant. The analogy does not work exactly the way the advocates of letting the baby cry might think. For a basket of fruit to spoil, you have to leave it alone on the shelf and let it rot. So it follows that children whose cries are not promptly responded to are more likely to be "spoiled." In fact, you can tell people who fear that prompt responses to a baby's crying will turn her into a clingy, whiney child that research has shown the opposite. Classic child development studies (Bell and Ainsworth 1972; 1977) show that children whose mothers had responded promptly to their cries as infants were less likely to use crying as a mode of communication at one year of age. These children were more likely to develop other social signals such as gestures, facial expressions, and vocalizations to communicate with their parents.

Parents are led to believe that if they pick up their baby every time she cries, she will not learn to settle

Babies nurse for comfort as well as for nourishment.

herself and will become more demanding as time goes on. This is not true. A baby whose cries have been promptly responded to early on learns to trust and to anticipate that a response will be forthcoming. As this baby gets older, usually around six months, that anticipation time gets longer, and both mother and baby are content to wait longer before activating and responding to the crying signal. Time invested early on gives you more time later.

Many studies have shot down the spoiling theory. Babies whose cries are not promptly responded to often learn to cry longer and with more disturbing cries. Studies have shown that mothers will often tend to interact less with babies who have prolonged disturbing cries. When these babies stopped crying as they got older, the mother still interacted less with these children. Why? The mothers had become insensitive to the babies' cries, and this insensitivity carried over into their later parent-child relationship. The advice to "let the baby cry" spoils the whole family.

Discipline. "You must discipline your baby" is another rationale for the "let your baby cry" advice. Unfortunately, discipline is often confused with parental control. Real discipline helps the child learn self-control. When parents stop a baby's crying by not listening to it, they not only squelch her signals, they squelch her initiative and they teach her to mistrust herself and others. In my opinion a parent first has to listen to the baby in order to help a baby gain control over herself. Unless the parents are open to the baby's signals, the baby cannot learn to play a part in her own discipline. This fear of letting the baby "be in control" keeps parents from laying the foundation of effective discipline: knowing their child and helping their child feel right.

Crying is good for babies. "It's good exercise for her lungs," say the advisors who have circulated this idea. Studies show absolutely no beneficial effect of crying, certainly not of prolonged crying. In one study, during unresponded-to crying episodes, babies' heart rates went up to worrisome levels (over 200 beats per minute), and oxygen levels in the blood dropped (Dinwiddie 1979). As soon as these crying infants were soothed, their cardiovascular systems rapidly returned to normal. Even the heart of a baby cries to be comforted. Crying is as good for the lungs as bleeding is for the veins. Babies who are left to cry it out by themselves can develop hoarseness that lasts for several days.

Another piece of erroneous medical folklore states that crying signifies a healthy baby. After birth a baby gets two extra points on her Apgar score for "crying lustily." I have observed and examined thousands of newborns right after birth and have come to believe that the state of quiet alertness is more beneficial to the baby than crying lustily. Crying is so "good" for toddlers that they often hold their breath and faint when a crying spell gets out of control. Besides being of no benefit to the lungs, recurrent unattended-to crying episodes may be detrimental to

"But I Did Everything Right"

" Thirteen months ago I gave birth to a baby boy. I had read a lot of books. I had been teaching childbirth classes and had prepared myself thoroughly. I had a healthy pregnancy with little stress, an excellent diet, and lots of exercise. I had an easy labor using the Bradley relaxation methods. We stayed at the clinic for two hours after the birth, and then the three of us went home. I did everything right. Alex slept next to me and nursed all night. I 'wore' him in the baby carrier, responded to his cues, and nursed on demand. I expected to have a calm, serene transition to motherhood. I was extremely confident.

"Alex turned out to be a colicky baby, screaming every evening for three to five hours. He never napped and cried whenever I put him down. He didn't like the carrier, went on a nursing strike at two months, had three tantrums at four months, screamed when we went anywhere in the car, and wouldn't touch a bottle. My confidence turned to self-doubt and despair. My friends all took a much more rigid approach with their children, and they criticized me frequently, telling me I was raising a monster who was too dependent on me and was trying to control my life. That was hard to take. I was a very confused mother.

" I know I am past a lot of this now with Alex, but with my next baby I'm going to have the real confidence I lacked before. Also, I plan to have new friends. I am now seeking out other mothers who have chosen to meet their children's needs as I have. I know my friends meant well, but they didn't help me at all."

> **Dr. Sears comments:** *The important point of this letter is the statement "I did everything right." This mother did not cause her baby's fussiness. Even "right from the start" babies fuss. It's important to surround yourself with friends who share your mothering style. Otherwise you can become confused because your friends can erode your confidence.*

the baby's development, perhaps because baby must divert so much energy into self-soothing (Torda 1976).

How the "cry it out" advice affects the mother

Mothers find the "let your baby cry" advice confusing. It goes against a mother's own intuition. A baby is not designed to be left to cry and the mother is not designed to let the baby cry. Mothers, your baby's cry and your responsive feeling is a unique mother-baby communication network designed for the survival of the young and the education of the parent. Ignore any advice that interferes with this communication network and doesn't feel right to you. Some new mothers are a bit shaky in trusting their own intuition over the advice of "experts." They may even feel guilty for not following the advice; love for their babies makes them vulnerable to any suggestions they might not be doing the right thing for the baby. I believe that trusted advisors should not be confusing new mothers like this.

Desensitizes mothers. Restraining her responses desensitizes the new mother to her baby. The "let the baby cry" advice encourages mothers not to listen to their baby or to their instincts. Some child care books in the past even contained the admonition, "Mothers, harden your hearts." If a mother continues to listen to someone else's advice instead of her own instincts and continues to ignore her baby's cues, she learns not to trust either herself or her baby. This will get her into trouble. She will become insensitive toward her baby and less confident as a parent.

How the "cry it out" advice affects the baby

Not responding to a baby's cries undermines trust. The development of a trusting relationship with a primary caretaker sets the pattern for the baby's future relationships with others. A child learns to trust as she is trusted. The more an infant trusts her own early crying cues, the more motivated she is to develop better communication skills. The more she trusts that a caregiver will respond, the better she will feel about trusting others in the years to come.

One day on a radio talk show, I explained why parents should not leave babies alone to cry it out. The next day one of my patients brought her five-year-old boy, Timothy, into my office. The mother told me, "We heard you on the radio yesterday. When you told the story about how sad a child was whose parents were leaving him cry in his crib alone, Timothy said, 'That poor little boy. I remember when you and Dad left me to cry.'"

"But it works." Yes, some crying babies will eventually get worn out, will give up, and will fall asleep. The "cry it out" advice may work with the easy, self-soothing baby (although there are good reasons for not allowing easy babies to cry it out). It seldom "works" for the high-need baby. In my questioning of several hundred parents nearly all said they couldn't let their babies cry; the majority of those who tried it said it didn't work. Remember the mother who restrained herself from giving a nurturing response to her baby's cry? The baby kept right on crying and got angrier and angrier. The mother herself said, "I'll never do that again." Her guilt and the baby's anger revealed that something had gone amiss in the previously trusting mother-baby communication network.

It may seem as if the non-responding (I think it's a non-responsible) approach makes sense. If a behavior is not reinforced or responded to, it goes away, a phenomenon that psychologists refer to as extinction. But what is it that goes away when you consistently fail to respond to baby's cries? Baby's ability to communicate is on the road to extinction, along with baby's trust in caregivers. I have great difficulty understanding this approach. By not giving in to your baby's cries, you teach your baby to give up, to despair. Both of you wind up losing.

Comforting is not controlling

I believe that there is a strong case against letting the baby "cry it out." I hope that my advice will help babies cry better and help parents listen better. This doesn't mean that you will always be able to stop your baby's crying or that you must pick your baby up and comfort her every time she makes a peep. There will be times when your baby will cry and nothing you do in response seems to work. It's important for you to be there with your baby, but don't feel that you must *make* her stop crying. Comforting a baby is not about control.

As babies get older, mothers learn when to wait a few minutes before coming to the rescue. The baby noises that go along with "I'm working this out for myself" don't have the same urgency as crying. If you respond to them anxiously, rushing in to help baby resolve her problem, she may conclude that she really can't act independently. She will pick up on your anxiety and become overcautious and worried instead of more confident of her abilities. Your job as a parent is to help your baby learn what she needs to know to be happy and successful. When she is just a few weeks old, she needs to learn that her distress will be followed by comfort. Later—and a sensitive, responsive mom is the best judge of when this is—she will be ready to learn that she can tolerate a few minutes of frustration as she struggles with new challenges.

*"Nobody
Picked Me
Up"*

" I have always wondered how much of my mothering
efforts my baby will remember when he is older. The
following story has convinced me that my mothering
does indeed have long-term effects.

" A twenty-two-year-old friend of mine recently tried
to commit suicide. During intense psychoanalysis
following her attempt, she revealed a flashback from
when she was a tiny baby lying alone in her crib,
crying helplessly. She broke down into tears, crying.
'I felt so alone, and nobody would pick me up.'"

Dr. Sears comments: *Memory researchers believe that
we never completely forget anything; all events, especially
traumatic ones, are permanently imprinted in our minds.
I believe that high-need babies, because of their supersensitivity may have particularly vivid memories.*

Survival Tips

Since crying is a language involving both a talker (the baby) and
a listener (usually the mother), survival tips can be directed
at both members of the crying communication network. You
can learn how to minimize the disturbing qualities of your
baby's cries by training her to cry better. You can also build up
your sensitivity to and tolerance of your baby's cries. Here are
some survival tips aimed at mellowing your baby's behavior and
your own.

A peaceful postpartum period

Many babies do not show fussy behavior until around two weeks of age when the more disturbing crying seems to begin. I call this the two-week grace period. It's as if some babies are born potentially fussy, but they give their caregivers a two-week opportunity to mellow their temperaments. If the babies don't receive the help they need, the fussing begins.

Most babies, however, show their true colors soon after birth. You can usually spot a high-need baby even as a newborn. Right after birth the baby's behavior says, "Hi, Mom and Dad, I'm an above-average baby, and I need above-average parenting. If you give it to me, we're going to get along fine. If you don't, we're going to have a bit of trouble down the line."

Mellowing the baby's cries should begin immediately after birth as parents and baby spend some time together, getting to know one another. In the first hour or two after birth, babies enter a state of quiet alert. They gaze at the world around them and seek out the eyes and other features of parents' faces. It's a time when mom and dad can get positively hooked on their new baby, and baby can learn to feel peaceful and at home, cuddled and supported in dad's arms or at mom's breast.

Rooming-in during the time mother and baby are in the hospital continues this bonding process. Studies have shown that both mother and baby profit from rooming-in together. Infants of rooming-in mothers cry less. Mothers who room-in exhibit more mature coping skills with their crying babies postpartum (Greenberg 1973). The infant distress syndrome (fussiness, colic, incessant crying) is more common in infants delivered in hospitals where babies are kept in central nurseries rather than with their mothers (Craven 1979).

Imagine the first days of life for a baby kept in a hospital nursery, away from her own mother. The newborn infant lies in a plastic box. She awakens hungry and turns her head, looking for something to eat. Maybe she finds her fist and sucks on it for a few seconds. Soon she grows more anxious and starts to whimper and cry, along with twenty other hungry babies in plastic boxes who have all managed to awaken each other. A caregiver who has no biological attachment to the baby—no inner programming tuned to that baby—hears the early attachment-promoting cries and responds when she gets a chance. The crying, hungry baby is taken to the mother for feeding. By this time, baby may be "over the hill" on the crying curve or so upset that she has given up, shut down, and withdrawn into sleep.

The mother, meanwhile, has missed the opening scene in this biological drama because she was not present in the nursery when her baby first cried. She hasn't seen the early hunger signals and hasn't heard the appealing whimpers that would make her pick up this baby who needs her. Instead, she is expected to give a nurturing response to a baby whose behavior—intense disturbing cries or a sound sleep—makes her feel as if her baby doesn't like her. When mother has to wait for others to bring her baby to her from the other end of the maternity unit, she hears only cries that are likely to elicit agitated concern or even an avoidance response. So even though she has a biological attachment to the baby and a comforting breast to offer, she is tied up in knots. Her baby is too tense to breastfeed well, her milk won't let down, and the baby cries even harder. The mother feels like a failure as the "experts" in the nursery take over with a bottle of formula. This leads to more separation, more missed cues, more breaks in the attachment between mother and baby. They may leave the hospital together, but they arrive home feeling like strangers.

Contrast this with the rooming-in baby. She awakens in her mother's room, maybe in her arms. Her pre-cry hunger signals are promptly attended to and she is put to the breast even before she needs to cry. If the baby does cry, it is the initial attachment-promoting cry. When given a prompt nurturing response, this cry never has a chance to develop into a disturbing cry. The attachment-promoting cry elicits a hormonal response in the mother, her milk lets down, and the mother and infant are in biological harmony. Nursery babies cry harder, but rooming-in babies learn to cry better in the first days after birth.

Unrestricted feeding schedules

Rigid feeding routines lead to excessive and unnece_ crying (Bernal 1979). Feeding babies whenever they show signs of hunger prevents hunger cries from turning into more disturbing cries. As the American Academy of Pediatrics (1997) put it in their statement recommending breastfeeding, "Crying is a late indicator of hunger."

Babies nurse for comfort as well as for nourishment; sometimes they want some "dessert" fifteen or twenty minutes after they've finished "dinner." Making babies wait until a set time to eat makes little sense—especially when you remember that babies not only can't tell time, they don't understand concepts like "soon" or "wait." Following your baby's hunger cues, rather than checking the clock, will help to minimize and mellow out her crying.

Carry your baby

Get used to "wearing" your baby. Babies who are carried a lot cry less. One study showed that three extra hours of carrying a day reduced the amount babies cried by forty-five percent (Hunziker and Barr 1986). Most babies feel content when they are in the arms of a parent. They enjoy the motion, the security of being held, the feeling that their arms and legs are contained and controlled rather than flailing around in space. If your high-need baby is happiest in your arms, don't waste energy trying to get her to enjoy her crib or infant seat. Learn to use a baby sling and enjoy the closeness.

Develop your sensitivity

When your baby fusses or cries, don't stop and think, "Why is she crying? What does she want from me? Is she trying to manipulate me? Am I being taken advantage of? Am I spoiling her?" If you feel must analyze your response to your baby's cries, at least wait until after you have responded. Restraining yourself from responding to your baby's cries until you have figured out exacty what's going on simply won't work. Mother-baby communication is more an art than a science. A baby's cry is a baby's own unique language. No two babies cry the same, nor are any two mother-baby communication units wired alike. To develop your sensitivity you must be open to your baby's cries and not restrain your responses. Take a risk. Your first impulse will probably be the right one. And if it's not, your baby has still received some kind of response to her complaints, which will encourage her to keep communicating.

Some mothers will confess, "But I just don't feel like I have any intuition. I really don't know why my baby is crying." It isn't as important to know why your baby is crying as it is to simply respond to your baby. I strongly believe that there is within each mother a built-in radar system—her intuition—that will eventually be fine-tuned to her baby. The key to the fine-tuning is to create the conditions which allow this inner consciousness to develop. Being open to your baby's cries and responding to them immediately allow this intuition to develop. Restrained responses hinder the development of intuition. Some mothers take a little longer to develop this crying sensitivity, and some babies take a little longer to respond to a mother's comforting measures, but the two of you will work things out as long as you let the communication flow as it is designed to do.

When I use the word intuition, I don't mean some mysterious form of parental extra-sensory perception that is activated when a child is conceived or born. Intuition comes from an accumulation of experience, lots of little insights and observations gained from all the time you spend with your baby and the many ways in which you respond to her needs. Using your mother's intuition is like riding a bike—you learn to do it without thinking about each little adjustment you make to stay balanced and moving forward.

Building up your sensitivity chemistry. Breastfeeding mothers have high levels of a hormone called prolactin. This is sometimes referred to as the mothering hormone. While science has yet to demonstrate that it affects humans' mothering behaviors (which are very complex), we do know that prolactin helps the body deal with stress, and research has shown that breastfeeding mothers are more tolerant of stress. I have also referred to this hormone as the perseverance hormone—it can help you stay calm and keep working at mothering your baby.

Prolactin is released when your baby sucks at your breast. Levels of prolactin rise during breastfeeding. It is the frequency of sucking, even more than the intensity, that has the greatest effect on prolactin levels. Thus, unrestricted breastfeeding builds up your prolactin. The calm, relaxed feelings that mothers experience during nursing sessions, thanks to prolactin and the other breastfeeding hormone, oxytocin, are nature's way of rewarding mothers for caring for their babies.

Spending more time with your baby also increases your sensitivity. Touching, grooming, and just snuggling up close to your baby will help you get to know her. Looking at your baby, talking to her, having eye-to-eye contact, and sleeping with your baby are other ways of nourishing your intuition. Don't wait for your baby to cry and become upset before you pick her up. Lots of positive contact with your baby—just because you love her— will build up your reserves of patience and caring for the times when crying and fussing make her seem less than lovable.

Your after-cry feeling. From time to time you might want to examine how you feel after you have responded to your baby's cries without restraint. I think that within each mother there is an internal sensor. She feels right when she responds correctly and feels wrong when she does not. Picture yourself as having an internal electronic sensor with several response lights. One is labeled, "Red alert: jump up and respond immediately." Another light is labeled, "Hold off a bit." Still another light is for a response somewhere in between the first two. If your baby cries and your response corresponds to the sensor light that is lit, you experience an inner feeling of rightness. If your baby goes to "red alert," but you don't respond quickly because of interference from outside ("My mother-in-law told me I'm spoiling her"), the result is an internal feeling of "not right." The guilt light goes on, and you vow to pay closer attention to the sensor the next time.

A sensitive mother of a high-need baby told me the following story: "My baby was wearing me down. So one night when he woke up with his usual demanding cry at 3:00 AM, I decided to let him cry it out. Boy, was he mad! I'll never do that again. I felt guilty. His crying was bad for both of us." I responded, "You have developed a healthy guilt system. This means that you are well on your way to becoming a sensitive mother." When it comes to responding to your baby's cries, no one else can read the sensors for you. Your maternal sensors are uniquely sensitive to your own baby.

The ultimate in sensitivity. A mother whose baby had been all but glued to her since birth told me, "My baby seldom cries. She doesn't need to." The ultimate in sensitivity to your baby is to be so tuned-in to your baby's cues that she does not have to cry to get what she needs. You and your baby may not be this tuned-in to each other all the time, but as your baby learns to signal better and you build up your sensitivity, you will spend more time enjoying your baby and less time wondering what it is she needs.

Mothers and fathers who practice attachment parenting are tuned into their baby's stress indicators and will often respond before the crying starts. The older the infant the easier it is to read the signals. When a two-year-old looks up at you with raised arms, she is clearly sending a "Pick me up" message. Ignore this opening cue and you'll soon hear some whimpering.

If you still don't respond, this whimper develops into an all-out cry. I have never had a particularly high tolerance for babies' cries, so I tend to pay attention to that opening cue. Attached parents find life easier when they create a sensitive environment in their home so that babies seldom have to cry loud and long, if at all, to get what they need.

When Crying Becomes Hard to Handle

One reason cries get responses is because they have a disturbing effect on the listener. The mother especially is likely to feel, "I can't stand to hear him cry any longer." A cry cries to be turned off. The ideal cry is disturbing enough to elicit attachment or comforting behaviors, but not so disturbing as to put off the listener. Cries are primarily attachment-promoting behaviors which draw mothers and babies closer. The cries of a baby stimulate empathy in the parent; that is, the parent shares in the baby's emotionally painful state.

However, the incessant cries of a fussy baby may begin to have a negative or alienating effect on the mother. Parents of a fussy baby may get tired of "feeling for that baby." The strong love between parent and child makes parents particularly vulnerable to the stress of these empathetic feelings. If you know that you have a fussy baby or even think that you may have a fussy baby, realize that you start out at a higher risk of developing an unhealthy interpretation of your baby's cries. Studies have shown that mothers who perceive their infants as difficult early on and who are more restrained in their responses to the baby's cries are less likely to engage in reciprocal vocalization with their babies later on (Shaw 1977). In other words, they don't learn to enjoy their babies. In general, caregivers tend to misjudge the cries of fussy babies more often than those of easy babies. They are also more likely to call a difficult baby "spoiled." This may be a protective response to the stress of baby's cries constantly tugging on parental heartstrings.

"I Feel So Guilty"

"Shut up and leave me alone," screamed Janet at her four-month-old baby who had been crying for hours. Later she reported, "I feel so guilty about yelling at him."

Dr. Sears comments: *Janet's ambivalent feelings are shared by thousands of mothers of high-need babies. A mother's love and concern for her high-need baby make her particularly vulnerable to feelings which shatter her image of herself as a perfect mother. Even though she is not acting on her angry emotions, Janet feels guilty because good mothers aren't supposed to feel angry at their babies. This belief is not true.*

Mothers can get themselves in a real anger bind. They may feel angry toward their babies for being so difficult and not responding to comforting measures. They feel angry at themselves for not being able to comfort their fussy babies, and they get even angrier with themselves because they feel angry with their babies. Every mother I have ever counseled feels angry at her baby at some time. This anger stems from frustration at not being able to get through to the baby. It can also be the product of disappointment because the baby you got was not the happy, peaceful baby you expected. It's important to recognize when you feel angry. Janet's feelings of guilt are a normal reflection of her love and sensitivity toward her baby, but it's also important for Janet to recognize and acknowledge her anger. Talking about it with a sympathetic husband or a trusted friend will help.

Because of the fussy baby's nature, her cues are more intense. The increased intensity of these cries may initially promote more intense responses. However, these intense cries may also become increasingly disturbing, resulting in what I call the "over-the-hill" response. The person on the receiving end of the cries gets overloaded, and the cries begin to provoke an avoidance response. A certain amount of avoidance is normal and healthy; it preserves your sanity. But a pattern of increasing avoidance and decreasing responsiveness is an early warning sign of a disturbance in the mother-infant relationship. It may be a time to seek professional help from someone who understands why babies cry, what mothers can do to comfort them, and how mothers can care for themselves so that they can better handle the stress of caring for a fussy baby. Talk to your pediatrician, seek out a support group, such as La Leche League, or talk to a counselor who has experience treating new mothers.

Fussy babies and child abuse

One day when I was counseling parents of a high-need baby, the mother inadvertently referred to her baby as a high risk baby. In a way, she was right. High-need babies have a higher risk of being abused.

The ideal cry is powerful enough to elicit a sympathetic response from the caregiver, yet is not so disturbing as to trigger either an avoidance response or anger. Incessant disturbing crying can provoke child abuse. An analysis of cases of child abuse provoked by crying showed that the communication network had already broken down in these parent-child relationships (Ounsted 1974):

- Parents who battered their babies were more likely to have practiced a style of parenting characterized by restrained responses.
- These parents were more likely to label their babies as "difficult."

- The battered babies generally had a more disturbing quality to their cries.

The communication network broke down because the babies' cries were not responded to promptly from early infancy. These babies learned to cry harder instead of to cry better. As a result the cries became more disturbing and released angry emotions rather than sympathy in a parent already at risk of being abusive.

Early counseling and coaching might have trained these parents to understand the signal value of their infants' cries. Their babies could have learned to cry more effectively, right from the start. The baby's cries would then trigger empathic responses in the parent rather than releasing the parent's anger. The prevention of child abuse is just another example of the good that can happen when parents and babies learn to listen to each other.

REFERENCES

American Academy of Pediatrics Work Group on Breastfeeding. 1997. Breastfeeding and the use of human milk. *Pediatrics* 100:1035.

Bell, S. M. and Ainsworth, M. D. 1972. Infant crying and maternal responsiveness. *Child Dev* 43:1171.

_____. 1977. Infant crying and maternal responsiveness: A rejoiner to Gewintz and Boyd. *Child Dev* 48:1208.

Bernal, I. 1972. Crying during the first 10 days of life and maternal responses. *Dev Med Child Neurol* 14:362.

Dihigo, S. K. 1998. New strategies for the treatment of colic: Modifying the parent/infant interaction. *J Pediatr Health Care* 12:256.

Dinwiddie, R. et al. 1979. Cardiopulmonary changes in the crying neonate. *Pediatr Res* 13:900.

Greenberg, M. et al. 1973. First mothers rooming in with their newborn: Its impact upon the mother. *Am J Orthopsychiatr* 43:783.

Hunziker, U. and Barr, R. 1986. Increased carrying reduces infant crying: A randomized controlled trial. *Pediatrics* 77:641.

Ounsted, C. et al. 1974. Aspects of bonding failure: The psychopathology and psychotherapeutic treatment of families of battered children. *Dev Med Child Neurol* 16:447.

Torda, C. 1976. Effects of postnatal stress on visual and auditory evoked potential. *Perceptual Motor Skills* 43:315.

Vuorenkoski, V. et al. 1969. The effect of cry stimulus on the temperature of the lactating breast of primipara: A thermographic study. *Experientia* 25:1286.

Wolke, D. et al. 1994. Excessive infant crying: A controlled study of mothers helping mothers. *Pediatrics* 94:322.

CHAPTER FIVE

Parenting the Colicky Baby

If you are wondering whether or not you have a colicky baby, you probably don't have one. The colicky baby leaves no doubt in the minds of sympathetic caregivers that he is truly in agony. Something is hurting him, and his cries along with his body language make that plain. This type of crying is not easily soothed by picking baby up, holding him, feeding him, or walking with him. I prefer to describe a baby others may call colicky as a "hurting baby." This motivates mothers, fathers, and physicians to find a way to alleviate baby's pain, rather than shrugging their shoulders and saying, "It's just colic."

There is a large overlap between babies who are fussy and babies who are colicky. In this book I refer to screaming babies as colicky or as hurting babies if the cries seem to have primarily physical causes and as fussy if the cries stem primarily from baby's temperament. Be aware that a baby who is hurting or colicky may fuss for other reasons too, and fussy babies experience psychological distress with an urgency similar to physical pain.

I want to emphasize right at the outset that what you do about a baby's cries—whether fussy or colicky—is more important than what you call them.

How many babies have colic? It is difficult to assess the true incidence of colic since "excessive crying" means different things to different parents and researchers. Most studies claim that from twelve to sixteen percent of all babies experience some colic episodes during the first six months. The incidence of both colicky and fussy babies (babies who cry a lot) is around twenty-five percent.

Profile of a Colicky Baby

The kind of crying that physicians describe as colic is not a disease; it is a syndrome—a collection of symptoms. A colicky baby screams from intense physical discomfort. He draws his legs up onto a tense abdomen and clenches his fists, seemingly angry at having this uncontrollable pain. The colicky baby communicates to his parents that he is in pain, but they feel as helpless as he does at determining the cause of and alleviating the hurt. The violent and agonizing quality of the colic cry drives parents to the edge. The cry of a colicky baby is paroxysmal, which means it occurs in sudden and unexpected outbursts. Bewildered parents will often say, "He seemed perfectly happy and content just a minute ago. Now he's a wreck."

Frequent "ouch" signs are characteristic of colic's pain cries. The most disturbing feature of the colic cry is the body language that accompanies it: anger, muscle tension, flailing of arms and legs, clenched fists, facial grimaces, and a hard tummy. The baby's arms are clenched tightly close to his chest and his knees are drawn up so tightly they nearly bump his abdomen. Periodically during these attacks the infant may throw out his arms, stiffen his back, arch his neck, and dart out his legs, a move resembling a frantically executed back dive. Babies often fall into a deep sleep after the colicky episode is over.

The unrelenting nature of colic attacks is what usually gets to parents. Colicky spells may last a few minutes to a few hours, with occasional pauses of calm before the next storm breaks. By some perverse quirk of justice, colic seldom occurs in the morning when parents and infant are well rested; it usually occurs in late afternoon or early evening when parental reserves are lowest. In contrast to fussy high-need babies who fuss all day, some colicky babies are relatively easy to handle when they're not having colicky periods. One mother told me, "He seems like two different babies, Dr. Jekyll and Mr. Hyde." On the positive side, colicky babies are the picture of good health. They tend to eat more and grow faster than non-colicky babies. The thriving appearance of the colicky baby often causes onlookers to remark, "My what a healthy looking baby. You're so lucky." Worn-out mothers respond, "You should have seen us a few hours ago."

Medical researchers have attempted to come up with a uniform definition of colic so that they can more accurately compare the results of studies of colic. Here's the classic definition of colic:

- Occurs in otherwise healthy, thriving infants
- Paroxysms of inconsolable crying without any identifiable physical causes
- Begins within the first three weeks
- Lasts at least three hours a day, three days per week, and continues for at least three weeks.

I find that colic symptoms vary widely from baby to baby and from day to day in the same baby. What makes it colic is that the baby seems to be in pain.

What Colic Is Not

The most frustrating part of parenting the colicky type of high-need baby is that it can be very difficult to determine the cause of a particular baby's colic attacks. Parents, pediatrician, and wise grandmothers may weigh in with opinions, but they may only be guessing. This has a significant effect on the parents' sympathy for a colicky baby. It is much easier to put in the effort to comfort a person who is hurting when there is a readily identifiable medical cause for the hurt, a cause you can do something about. Not knowing what is wrong is very frustrating. While colic usually brings out a sympathetic response from parents, it can also make them wonder just what this baby wants from them. These exasperated feelings may compel the caregiver to distance herself a bit from baby's crying, and this may result in less-nurturing responses.

The term colic means an acute, sharp pain in the abdomen. Because this pain was originally thought to be caused by gas in the colon, it was labeled "colic." There are many popular ideas about the causes of colic. Many of them are only myths; they do not stand up to a critical look.

"Oh, he's just full of gas!"

In the long and often fruitless search for the cause of colic, gas often gets the blame. During colicky periods, the infant's tummy does seem more distended, and he passes a lot of flatus. Colicky babies often have many stools each day (probably because they eat so much). At other times, mothers will often notice small amounts of stool in the diaper that has accompanied the forced expulsion of air.

X-ray studies cast doubt on the theories that intestinal gas is the culprit in colic (Paradise 1966). Abdominal x-rays of non-colicky infants frequently reveal a lot of distention of the intestines with gas, but the infants do not seem to be uncomfortable. X-rays taken during and after colic crying spells showed no gas during the crying episode but a lot of gas afterwards. Air is gulped and swallowed during crying. Distention of the intestines by gas may be the result rather than the cause of colicky crying.

Pain cries and anger cries are likely to be accompanied by

the swallowing of air. These cries have a very long exhalation phase, ending in a "blue period" of voiceless crying. Then the baby takes a big, gulping breath, as if he is trying to catch up on the breathing he was unable to do while he was howling. This sudden gasping may cause air to enter the stomach as well as the lungs. The air then accumulates in the intestines as gas, and colic results.

This is why a prompt response to crying is important, especially in infants with a low pain threshold. Helping the infant stop crying may lessen the amount of air the baby swallows, thus decreasing the amount of intestinal gas and shortening the duration of the colic cry. Those infants who are truly gassy babies need their parents to help them learn to cry better and more efficiently, so that they are less at risk for swallowing air. A prompt response is the first step in doing this.

The tense mother/tense baby syndrome

Colicky behavior in the infant is sometimes unjustly blamed on the mother. Some observers claim that the mother transfers her own anxiety to the baby, and the baby reacts accordingly. In most cases of colic, this just isn't true. Colic occurs in babies of accepting, easygoing mothers as well as in babies whose mothers are more prone to be anxious. This is an important point because the behavior of the baby is often unjustly interpreted as a reflection of the "goodness" of the mother. It is true that mothers vary widely in their coping abilities and that colic, like any stress that is not quickly dealt with, can be prolonged and reinforced by the mother's anxiety. While some studies have shown that mothers who are tense, anxious, and depressed during their pregnancy are also more likely to have colicky babies, others have shown absolutely no correlation between the personality of the mother and colicky behavior of the baby (Carey 1968). Some studies also show that colic may be the result of a self-fulfilling prophecy. Mothers who expect to have trouble with their babies are more likely to have fussy babies. This may indicate that these mothers are less accepting of their infant's needs and less likely to provide the comfort these babies are asking for.

It is important to remember that most of the mothers in these studies who rated themselves as anxious did not turn out to have fussy babies. In my opinion, the emotional make-up of the mother has more influence on how she handles her colicky baby than it does on whether the baby has colic. Some mothers are better than others at keeping their cool while trying to comfort their baby. A tense baby doesn't settle well in tense arms.

"It must be your milk"

Most studies show no difference in the colic incidence between breastfed and formula-fed babies; however in my experience, breastfeeding mothers often exhibit better coping skills. No matter what some ill-informed advisor may say about your milk, it's not what's causing your baby's colic. Weaning to formula won't help, although you might consider whether something in your diet is bothering your baby. (See the section on food intolerance on pages 82 and 117.)

What Is Causing the Pain?

When baby is hurting, both parents and pediatrician want to find out why. Colicky crying should not be dismissed as something baby "will grow out of" or a phase that parents must simply endure. If your fussy baby continues to cry angrily, as if in pain, despite your best efforts to comfort and quiet him, you need to talk to your doctor. Here are some of the causes of crying that your doctor will consider.

Gastroesophageal reflux

Babies with gastroesophageal reflux (GER) may fuss and have crying spells that masquerade as colic. Babies with GER regurgitate stomach acids into the esophagus, which produces an uncomfortable burning sensation that adults would describe as heartburn. I'm convinced that many babies dismissed by earlier generations of parents and physicians as "colicky" actually had reflux. Only in the last ten years have physicians come to appreciate this problem as a source of infant distress—one they can do something about.

GER is not always easy to diagnose. Some babies with GER spit up a lot; in others, the regurgitated liquid doesn't make it all the way up the esophagus and onto a parent's shoulder. Here are some signs that reflux may be what's bothering your baby:

- Colicky crying that begins shortly after a feeding
- Night-waking and colicky crying that is soothed by feeding
- Spitting up during or shortly after feedings (though not all babies with GER spit up, and not all babies who spit up a lot have GER)
- Frequent respiratory infections.

Breastfed babies are less likely to have GER than formula-fed infants, and their symptoms may be less severe (Heacock 1992). Babies digest breast milk faster than formula. Since it stays in the stomach for a shorter time, there is less opportunity to regurgitate human milk.

Talk to your doctor if you suspect that your baby has GER. Your pediatrician may order tests to determine if your baby's colicky crying is caused by GER or may make a diagnosis based on your observations of your baby's behavior. The pediatrician may prescribe medication that neutralizes stomach acid and helps the stomach empty more quickly.

Keeping the baby with GER in an upright position for thirty minutes after a feeding gives gravity a chance to keep those stomach acids in the stomach and out of the esophagus. Hold baby upright over your shoulder until his stomach has a chance to settle and digest his meal. You can raise one end of baby's mattress at a thirty degree angle to help him sleep better. Babies with GER have an easier time if you offer smaller, more frequent feedings. Stomachs that are too full are more likely to send their contents back up the esophagus.

Food intolerance and colic

Sometimes colic is caused by food allergies. In my experience, babies with food allergies usually have more than one symptom—a rash on the cheeks or bottom, a runny nose, or diarrhea in addition to colic.

Though some formula-fed infants improve when switched to soy-based or predigested formulas, the search for the "right formula" is generally fruitless. Also, babies allergic to cow's milk are frequently allergic to soy formula as well. You should consult your doctor before switching a formula-fed baby from one kind of formula to another.

Colicky reactions in breastfed babies may be related to something in the mother's diet. Some food proteins are able to pass into mother's milk and may provoke an allergic reaction in a sensitive baby. If baby's fussiness and colicky crying are upsetting you and the whole family, investigating whether baby is sensitive to something in mother's diet is worth a try.

Common "fuss foods" include milk and other dairy products, nuts and peanut butter, and corn. Eliminate the foods you suspect from your diet for at least two weeks. (Be sure to read labels. Dairy products such as whey, casein, and sodium caseinate appear in many processed foods.) Do you see an obvious change in your baby's behavior?

Research has shown that cow's milk proteins from mother's diet do appear in her milk, and other studies have shown that when mother eliminates dairy products from her diet, fussy babies fuss less. Restricting mothers' diets while breastfeeding won't cure every case of colic, but eliminating milk for a couple of weeks is worth a try, especially if you or your partner has a family history of food allergy.

Do foods that make adults gassy produce gas in breastfed babies? I've found a discrepancy between mothers' reports and nutritional science. There is no scientific rationale for thinking that gas from foods the mother eats gets into her milk and produces gas in the baby. But occasionally a mother will tell me that she notices colicky symptoms in her baby within a few hours after eating certain foods. The foods most commonly reported as causing symptoms are:

- Raw vegetables: broccoli, cabbage, onions, green peppers, cauliflower
- Chocolate
- Eggs
- Shellfish
- Nuts
- Citrus fruits
- Synthetic vitamins (either mother's or baby's).

Some of the above are also common causes of food allergies.

Several mothers, who taste their own milk regularly, have told me that they have noticed a change in the taste of their milk after they have indulged in spicy ethnic foods. The taste change also coincided with a colicky period in their babies. The changing taste of human milk may be one of the ways babies learn to like the strong-flavored foods of their particular culture; they pick up on the flavor of garlic, curry, or chili in their mother's milk. Some babies may be more tolerant of this than others.

It can be helpful to keep a diary of what you eat each day, how much and when your baby fusses, and any other symptoms you observe in either baby or yourself. Manipulating your diet can be tricky, and the conclusions mothers draw are sometimes rather subjective. You may discover a predictable correlation between something you eat and your baby's fussy periods, or you may not. If you spend several weeks eliminating different foods from your diet and evaluating baby's behavior, baby may eventually stop fussing, but you won't be sure if baby is truly sensitive to chili peppers (or whatever) or if he has simply out-grown the colic problem. To establish a causal connection between food and fussing, you need to retry the food under sus-picion and see if the fussing recurs. Although the relationship between cow's milk, other allergens, and colic is not always clear, dietary manipulation in mother and baby is certainly worth a try, especially since colic can have such a devastating effect on the whole family. A note of caution: breastfeeding mothers who eliminate entire food groups (for example, dairy products) from their diet for more than two weeks might want to consult a dietitian for nutritional advice.

Foremilk/hindmilk imbalance

When breastfed babies get a steady diet of mother's lactose-rich foremilk and not enough of her high-fat hindmilk, they may get a tummy-ache and complain with colicky crying. This problem is easily managed. See Chapter 7, "Feeding the Fussy Baby," for suggestions.

Other medical problems

Common ailments of infancy can produce painful crying. If you think your baby is hurting, call the doctor. When a parent's intu-ition says a baby is in pain, wise pediatricians listen and look for the cause.

Ear infections. The symptoms of ear infections are frequently missed in colicky babies because they're passed off as another instance of "there he goes again." Keep in mind that most true colic does not awaken babies from sleep; ear infections do. In fact, they are worse at night because when a baby lies flat the infected fluid presses down on the sensitive eardrum. A baby who seems in pain when lying down but not when sitting up may have an ear infection. Cold symptoms such as a snotty nose, draining eyes, and a low grade fever often accompany the infection.

Be aware of signs of a perforated eardrum: Baby suddenly wakes up screaming during the night and then toward the morning seems better, but you notice some yellowish-white crusty fluid around the outside of the ear. The baby may seem more comfortable after the eardrum has perforated because the pressure is released, but you should still obtain medical attention. Remember that babies with ear infections often seem better the next morning because they are no longer lying down.

Diaper rash. Sudden outbursts of screaming may be caused by a sore bottom. The type of diaper rashes that are particularly distressing are the burnt, red, raw rashes caused by acid stools during diarrhea. A baking soda bath (one tablespoon baking soda in a couple inches of water in baby's bathtub) may soothe the diaper rash caused by acid stools.

Urinary tract infections. The most serious hidden cause of colic is urinary tract infection. These infections are subtle. They do not begin as quickly and severely as ear infections and can last several weeks before they are detected. Urinary tract infections can cause kidney damage if undetected and untreated. I believe that all fussy, colicky babies should have at least three urinalyses. When making your appointment for a fussy baby consultation, ask the doctor's assistant to mail you three urine bags so that you can bring in urine specimens on or before the day of your appointment.

Colic Communication Tips

Since most colic occurs outside of doctors' office hours, your doctor may not have the privilege of witnessing your baby's painful crying. When seeking professional help for your colicky or fussy baby, be honest with your doctor about two important points: how much the colic bothers your baby and how much it bothers you.

Here are some of the things you'll need to tell the doctor when discussing your baby's colic problems. Think about them ahead of time, and make a list to take with you to the doctor's office.

- When the colic episodes started, how often they occur, how long they last
- The time of the day and the circumstances around which they occur (at home, with care-givers other than mother, when the family is busy)
- What seems to turn the colic episodes on and what turns them off
- Where you feel the baby's pain is coming from, what his face, abdomen, and extremities look like
- A description of the cry
- Details about feeding: breast or bottle frequency, swallowing. Do you hear the baby gulping air?
- Nature of the baby's bowel movements: easy or straining, soft or hard, how frequent
- How much he passes gas
- Spitting up: how often, how soon after feeding, how much force
- What the baby's bottom looks like. A persistent diaper rash or a red burnt-looking bottom suggests some sort of food intolerance.
- What you have tried to do for the colic episodes—what worked and what didn't
- What your diagnosis is.

Be sure to tell your doctor what effect the colic is having on the whole family. I have discovered that is it not uncommon for mothers to open a conversation by telling me, "Our whole family is falling apart—me, my baby, and my marriage." Don't hesitate to tell the real story during the office visit. Don't minimize the problem. This gets the point across that your baby's colic bothers you.

If your doctor is unable to witness one of these colicky episodes, it may help to make a "distress tape," a recording of one of the baby's crying jags. I find it difficult, though, to truly appreciate an infant's cry from the sound only; there is so much that body language can tell you about the level of the baby's distress. If you really want to get the point across and you have the equipment (or can rent it) have your husband make a video tape of you and your baby during a colicky episode so that your counselor can truly witness a mother-infant pair in distress. Some parents find it very therapeutic to sit back and analyze a series of tapes of crying episodes as their infant grows older. When they look back, parents are often amazed at the complete turnabout in the baby's personality. As they look at or listen to some of the earlier distress tapes they often exclaim, "We've come a long way, baby!"

I find it particularly helpful to have parents keep some sort of diary that lists the time of day and the activity of the infant on one side of the page and the activity of the rest of the family on the other. You'll be surprised at correlations you'll discover. For example, I found that typical colic seldom awakens the baby during the night. Pain that awakens babies from sleep is more likely to have a physical than an emotional cause.

If possible, both mother and father should attend the office visit. The presence of the father keeps mothers honest. Mothers may sometimes play down how much their crying baby upsets them; they fear that such a revelation will shatter their perfect mother image in the eyes of the pediatrician. Fathers also may more readily volunteer how the fussy baby is affecting the overall dynamics of the family. One family came in for colic counseling with me, and I really didn't appreciate the severity of the problem until the father volunteered, "I had a vasectomy last week. We'll never go through this again." I got the picture.

Some Other Explanations for Colic

Every colicky baby deserves to have his pain taken seriously and investigated. However, a thorough medical exam will not always provide an explanation for baby's colicky outbursts. Here are some other factors that may contribute to persistent crying.

Smoking

Colic incidence is higher in infants whose mothers smoke. Colic incidence is also higher when fathers smoke (Said 1984), which suggests that colic may be related to the home environment rather than to a direct transfer of chemicals through the mother's milk. Studies have also shown that mothers who smoke have lower prolactin levels (Matheson 1989; Andersen 1982), which may affect their milk supply as well as decrease their ability to cope with colicky crying. If you can't quit, at least cut back on the number of cigarettes you smoke. And don't smoke in the same room as the baby.

Birth and colic

Events surrounding the birth may affect colic. The incidence of colic is higher in infants who are the product of a complicated and stressful birth and who have experienced a lot of mother-baby separation after birth. This goes along with the general tendency for infants to be fussy if they had a rough start and were separated from their mothers.

Biology and colic

Colic may be related to a neuro-developmental problem. This type of colicky baby belongs to the whole spectrum of fussy or high-need babies that come wired with a supersensitive, intense, disorganized, and slow-to-adapt temperament. Rather than fuss all the time, the colicky baby concentrates his fussiness toward the end of the day. There may be a biological explanation for this.

Disturbance in biological rhythms. Colic may be a disturbance in daily biological rhythms. The human body has daily fluctuations in sleep patterns, body temperature, and hormonal concentration. These daily peaks and valleys are called the circadian rhythm. In the first few months of a baby's life, these daily fluctuations are disorganized. By four to six months of age, the pattern becomes more regular. At the same time, the infant's sleep patterns become better organized, and colic subsides. Coincidence or cause and effect?

Hormonal problems. Progesterone is a hormone that can have calming and sleep-inducing effects. Before birth the baby receives progesterone through the placenta. The calming effect of maternal progesterone wears off in a week or two, and colic begins if the infant does not produce enough progesterone on his own. One study showed that colicky infants had low progesterone levels and that colic improved when treated with a progesterone-like drug (Clark 1963). Another study found no difference in progesterone levels in colicky and non-colicky infants (Weissbluth and Green 1983). This author, however, in another study grouped colicky infants together with infants of difficult temperaments or low sensory thresholds and concluded that "plasma progesterone levels were unusually low" in this group (Weissbluth 1983). Breastfed babies in this study had higher levels of progesterone. The significance of this finding is not clear, but it may help explain why some babies are fussier than others.

Prostaglandins have also been implicated in colic. These hormones cause strong contractions of intestinal muscles. In a study in which prostaglandins were used therapeutically to treat heart disease, the two infants involved developed colicky symptoms (Sankaran 1981).

The "colic hold" is often useful in soothing a fussy baby.

Problems adjusting to life outside the womb. Colic usually does not begin until after the second week of life. Could it be that during this grace period after birth there is something missing in the colicky infant's adjustment to life outside the womb? There is a tendency in our culture to view the newborn as a person separate from the mother, but perhaps the newborn doesn't feel that way. Is it possible that certain high-need babies need to be "glued" to their mothers for the first week or two after birth, nursed on demand, carried in arms, nestled next to the mother to sleep, and generally cared for in an organized, predictable, womb-like environment? If these infants do not get what they need and expect, they react with a behavior we call colic, which may be nothing more than the frustrated feelings of a baby who is not fitting well into his environment. I think that this may be a contributing factor in some, but not all, colicky babies. Even babies who have had the benefit of close attachment parenting from the moment of birth (I call them "right from the start" babies) get colic. Many of these babies are experiencing genuine pain, which should be investigated. Others may not have a hurting tummy, but may be less able to block out external stimuli. Once they get past the newborn sleepy period, they simply can't cope.

Why evening colic?

Another reason why I feel that colic is a neuro-developmental problem or even a hormonal problem is that it occurs most often in the evening hours, from 6:00-9:00 PM, the time of day some parents refer to as "the pits." If colic were caused by allergies, why would babies show this problem only three hours a day? While no one completely understands why colic occurs mainly in the evenings, there are some possible explanations.

Low parental reserves. Parents' reserves are lowest toward the end of the day. Babies couldn't time their colicky episodes more inconveniently. The colicky baby is upset just when most mothers are least able physically and emotionally to offer comfort. These babies need the most when parents are least able to give. By late afternoon or evening, most mothers are worn out by their babies' incessant demands. Even the most time-honored comforter, mother's breast, may not measure up to expectations at the end of the day. Levels of fat and protein in breast milk are lowest toward evening. Many mothers report a diminished milk supply toward the evening. Mothers also experience hormonal changes in the evening. Prolactin, which I call the perseverance hormone, is highest during sleep and in the morning hours. The blood level of cortisone is lowest around 6:00 PM, though how this affects maternal coping is not known.

Planning ahead for evening colic. Anticipate that you will spend the late afternoon and early evening with your baby in your arms. Plan ahead for evening colic by completing your household chores earlier in the day. Prepare the evening meal in the morning. Parents of colicky babies get used to casseroles that can be made ahead of time. It is wise to find ways to avoid chores

Many babies calm down quickly when held in the colic hold.

and commitments that will sap your energy during those evening colicky times.

Another way to plan ahead for evening colic is to encourage your baby to take a late afternoon nap. Around 4:00 PM, nestle up to your baby and nurse off to sleep together ("nap nursing"). Late afternoon napping and nursing helps both mother and baby: Mother gets a rest, a boost in her prolactin levels, and an energy recharge in preparation for the evening colic; baby's system also gets a rest at this crucial time before colic begins. Some mothers report that this late afternoon quiet time minimizes the frequency and severity of the evening colic.

When Will It Stop?

Colic begins around two weeks of age, peaks in severity between six and eight weeks, and is usually over by three to four months of age. Colic that persists beyond three to four months is likely to be caused by a medical problem such as milk intolerance.

Colic is at its worst at the period of an infant's development when he can do the least to comfort and amuse himself. During the first three months, babies are almost totally dependent on caregivers for stimulation. The severity of colic seems to lessen at a rate similar to the infant's development. I feel that the reason colic begins to subside around three months is that babies of that age can finally see clearly and are attracted by the visual delights and distractions around them. They can begin to do things with their hands and are learning self-soothing techniques such as finger-sucking, eye contact, and waving their arms and legs to let off steam. Around three months most babies show an increased maturity of the central nervous system, revealed by gradual organization of their sleep patterns. Also by the time the baby is two to three months old, most parents have become more adept at soothing techniques. But even though severe evening colicky episodes usually subside by six months, the general behavioral traits of the high-need baby may persist.

Some babies like eye contact; others prefer gentle patting on the back as you rock and croon to them.

Calming the Colicky Baby
The Colic Dance

Imagine ten mothers or fathers with colicky babies all dancing around at once, trying to soothe their little ones. One by one the tense babies drift off to sleep and melt into the arms of the parent. Every mother and father who has coped with a colicky baby has developed a unique rhythm, a dance motivated by love and desperation that keeps going until either the crier or the dancer wears down.

While each dance movement is as unique as a fingerprint, there are some common elements I have observed among all experienced dancers. They hold the baby firmly with a relaxed "I'm in charge" grasp and with as much skin-to-skin contact as possible. Nestled against mother's breast is usually the favorite embrace, but father's chest may provide an interesting change (which I call the "warm fuzzy").

The rhythm of the dance usually oscillates gently back and forth, alternating side-to-side and up-and-down motions. There's a lot of bending and straightening of the knees. The most successful rhythms are around seventy beats per minute (which corresponds to the pulse of uterine blood flow which the unborn baby has grown accustomed to). Gentle humming usually accompanies the dance; it sounds as if the mother is trying to approximate as closely as possible the sounds of the womb.

Fathers develop their own type of colic carry. The one that has worked best for me is to drape the baby stomach down over my forearm, her head in the crook of my elbow and legs straddling my hand. I grasp the diaper area firmly and my forearm presses on the baby's tense abdomen. The "warm fuzzy" position that I particularly enjoyed with our babies was to lie down and hold the baby securely with his head snuggled in my left armpit, his ear over my heartbeat and his cheek on my chest. The rhythm of the heartbeat plus the breathing movements will usually lull baby to sleep.

Another favorite snuggle is to dance neck-to-cheek. The baby snuggles his cheek into the groove between the parent's jaw and shoulder. In this position baby not only hears mom or dad's humming close to his ear but also feels the sound vibrations from the parent's jawbone all over his skull. This effect works especially well for dads, whose lower voices produce more noticeable vibrations.

Some babies prefer a lot of eye contact as you sing to them. Your baby may like to be held about a foot away from your face with one hand firmly under his bottom and the other firmly on his back. You can then bounce him rhythmically—fast or slow. This is a good way to get the baby to stop crying before going on to his favorite snuggling position. It is especially effective if you can make eye contact and croon baby's name. Don't feel destroyed if occasionally your baby does not respond to your comforting dance yet quiets down after an experienced friend or mother-in-law cuts in. Some experienced grandmothers have a very calming way of moving with babies.

You can develop a colic dance with your unborn baby. Some mothers of large families can often predict the temperament of a baby by activity in the womb. Mothers who have calmed their agitated unborn babies by songs and dances during pregnancy find that the same songs and dances work after birth.

Abdominal relaxation techniques

Sometimes warmth and gentle pressure on the abdomen helps soothe a colicky baby. Place baby tummy down on a half-filled warm water bottle that you have covered with a towel to protect the baby's skin. Letting baby fall asleep stomach down on a cushion with his legs dangling over the edge causes some soothing pressure to be applied to his belly. (However, once baby is sound asleep you should place him on his back. Sleeping on the stomach is associated with a higher risk of Sudden Infant Death Syndrome [SIDS]. Babies should not sleep stomach down or face down on cushions.) Some babies enjoy dad's large, warm hand pressing gently on their tummies; the palm should be over the navel and the fingers and thumb encircle baby's abdomen. Sometimes inserting a glycerin suppository into the baby's rectum with one hand while kneading baby's abdomen with the other will decompress a gas-filled abdomen.

Massaging baby's stomach. Infant massage is becoming quite an art among mothers of colicky babies. Here is a technique we have used in our babies.

Imagine a large "U" upside down on the baby's abdomen. This is the large intestine or colon along which the gas must pass, beginning on baby's right (your left), moving across his middle and down his left side until it exits through the rectum. By firmly and deeply massaging with your flattened fingers in a circular motion you can move gas pockets along this path. You can use the "I love you" method: Start with a single downward stroke for the "I" on baby's left side (see figure). This will move gas down and out of the last one-third of the colon. Then do the upside down "L" (the numeral 7 as you look at it) for the "love," moving gas along the middle segment and down the baby's left side. Finally, do the whole upside down "U" for the "you" as you

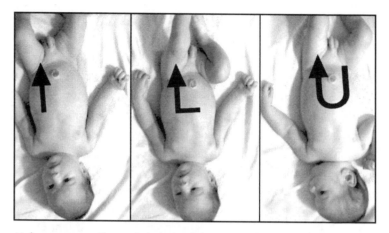

Help move gas through baby's abdomen with an "I Love You" massage.

stroke again up the baby's right side, across the middle segment, and down the left side. Baby must be relaxed for this massage to work, as a tense abdomen will resist the motion of your hands. Try it in a warm bath together or after some other comforting treatments. Warm oil on your hands will make massage easier.

The bubble bath. Use the abdominal massage technique while baby is in a warm bath. As baby passes the gas, bubbles will appear in the water.

Pacifiers

A general guideline for comforting the colicky baby would state that if it's safe and it works, use it. This is especially true with pacifiers, after the first month or so when nipple confusion is no longer a problem. (A pacifier nipple requires a different sucking action than mother's breast; this can confuse a tiny infant and contribute to problems with breastfeeding.) Some fussy babies need a large amount of non-nutritive sucking, and a pacifier fills the bill. Beware of using the pacifier as a mother substitute. The other end of a pacifier should always be attached to a person. A breast or a finger makes the best pacifier.

*More
Massage
Techniques*

"I tried warm baths with my baby. This helped, but
only as long as he was immersed in the warm water,
and realistically, you can't spend your life in a bath!
I also massaged his tummy while he was in the water.
With his feet toward me, I would place my left hand
across his middle and knead rather deeply with my
fingers concentrating on the left side close to the rib
cage. This helped some, but he only liked it when he
was in the water. After his bath I would rub him with
lotion, starting with his precious little feet and working up each leg. I found when I reached his thighs his
wails immediately turned into cackles of laughter.
I began to concentrate on massaging his thighs when
the colicky periods began, and even without the bath,
the reaction was always the same.

"The thigh massage I found most helpful went like
this. I would lay Eric in my lap on his back with
his head on my knee and his feet on my stomach.
I would place a hand on each thigh, thumb in the
groin area and fingers on the outside of the leg. Then
I would use a rather firm deep kneading motion with
equal pressure on both the inside and the outside of
the leg, squeezing, rolling, then releasing. It worked
every time, turning those pitiful wails into laughter—
at least for a while."

Respond promptly to baby's crying

In my experience the more promptly the cries of a colicky infant are attended to, the less he cries. The myth that parental over-responsiveness can reinforce the crying and produce so-called "trained crying" is erroneous. Both the experience of mothers and scientific studies have shown this theory to be false.

In fact, parental responsiveness can lessen the severity of colic. A study compared thirty colicky babies with thirty non-colicky babies (Taubman 1984). The colicky babies were divided into two groups. Parents in Group One were advised to use a restrained response to their infants, and were given the following suggestions:

- When infant crying continues despite all efforts to stop it, including feeding, do the following:
- Put the baby in the crib and let him cry for up to a half hour.
- If still crying, pick the baby up for a minute or so to calm him. Then return him to the crib.
- Repeat the above until the infant falls asleep or three hours have passed.
- After three hours the baby should be fed.

This advice was based on the hypothesis that babies cry no matter what the parents do and that overstimulation contributes to excessive crying. Group Two parents were advised to make immediate efforts to stop the crying and were given these instructions:

- Try to never let your baby cry.
- In attempting to discover why your infant is crying consider these possibilities:
    The baby is hungry and wants to be fed.
    The baby wants to suck, although he is not hungry.
    The baby wants to be held.

The baby is bored and wants stimulation.

The baby is tired and wants to sleep.

If the crying continues for more than five minutes with one response, then try another.

- Decide on your own in what order to explore the above possibilities.
- Don't be concerned about overfeeding your baby. This will not happen.
- Don't be concerned about spoiling your baby. This also will not happen.

This advice assumed that infants cry to express a need and they will continue to cry until the need is met. The study found that colicky infants cried an average of 2.6 (±1.0) hours per day, compared with 1.0 (±0.5) hour per day for non-colicky infants. After treatment with the restrained approach, the infants in Group One showed no decrease in daily crying time. After treatment with the responsive approach, the infants in Group Two cried 70 percent less. The crying decreased from 2.6 hours to 0.8 hours per day. It appears that a responsive parent-infant relationship can lessen colicky behavior in infants.

REFERENCES

Andersen, A. N. et al. 1982. Suppressed prolactin but normal neurophysin levels in cigarette smoking breastfeeding women. *Clin Endocrinol* 17:363.

Clark, R. L. et al. 1983. A study of the possible relationship of progesterone to colic. *Pediatrics* 32:65.

Heacock, H. J. et al. 1992. Influence of breast versus formula milk on physiological gastroesophageal reflux in health, newborn infants. *J Pediatr Gastroenterol* 14:41-46.

Matheson, I. et al. 1989. The effects of smoking on lactation and infantile colic. *J Am Med Assoc* 261:42.

Paradise, J. L. 1966. Maternal and other factors in the etiology of infantile colic. *J Am Med Assoc* 197:123

Said, G. et al. 1984. Infantile colic and parental smoking. *Br. Med J* 289:660.

Sankaran, K. et al. 1981. Intestinal colic and diarrhea as side effects of intravenous alprostadil administration. *Am J Dis Child* 135:664.

Taubman, B. 1984. Clinical trial of the treatment of colic by modification of parent-infant interaction. *Pediatrics* 74:998.

Weissbluth, M. 1983. *Crybabies.* New York: Arbor House.

Weissbluth, M. and Green, O. 1983. Plasma progesterone concentrations in infants: Relation to infantile colic. *J Pediatr* 103:935.

CHAPTER SIX

Soothing the Fussy Baby

"No one thing works all the time," complained a creative father who had collected a large repertoire of soothing techniques for his fussy baby. In this chapter I will share with you techniques that have worked in our own family and the many ideas which parents have related to me over the years.

Soothing techniques can be grouped into three general categories:

- Rhythmic motion
- Physical contact
- Soothing sounds.

Soothing the fussy baby is basically a matter of using "back to the womb" activities. Picture the womb environment of the fetus. She is in a free-floating fluid environment with which every square inch of her body is in contact; the fluid is at a constant temperature. Her hunger is automatically and continuous-ly satisfied, and the sounds around her are muted, calming, and rhythmic. Even when temporarily upset by her mother's anxi-eties or loud noises from the outside world, the fetus has the reassurance that her tranquil world will soon return to its usual predictability. The unborn baby gets accustomed to feeling right. Soothing techniques are all aimed at duplicating, as much as possible, the creature comforts that the baby has been pro-grammed prenatally to expect from her environment. If you have a high-need baby, you might consider the first three months after birth to be a fourth trimester of your pregnancy.

Moving in Harmony with Your Baby
Why motion is important to babies

Behind each ear is a tiny organ of balance called the vestibular system. This intricate system helps various parts of the body become aware of their relation to other parts and helps the body as a whole balance in space. The vestibular system is like three tiny carpenter's levels, one oriented for side-to-side balance, another for up-and-down, and the third for back-and-forth. They all function together to keep the body in balance. Every time you move, the fluid in these levels moves against tiny hair-like filaments which vibrate and send nerve impulses to the muscles in your body that will keep you in balance. For exam-ple, if you lean over too far to one side the vestibular system sig-nals that you should lean back to the other side to stay in bal-ance. The unborn baby has a very sensitive vestibular system which is constantly stimulated because the fetus is in almost continuous motion. This is why motion, not stillness, is the nor-mal state for a baby; a baby is born programmed to expect a stimulated vestibular system. The picture book baby lying qui-etly but alertly in her crib is a totally unrealistic expectation of how babies behave. The unborn baby also may not be accus-tomed to changes in gravity. This may explain why ultrasensitive babies have to be put down very slowly.

How to move with your baby

Because a newborn baby's vestibular system is accustomed to constant stimulation in three dimensions, the ideal rocking motion for soothing a fussy baby contains movements in all three planes, side to side, back and forth, and up and down. Rocking in a rocking chair

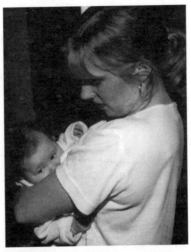

Motion is soothing for many fussy babies.

may soothe some babies, but it only stimulates the vestibular system in one plane, back and forth (with a small amount of up-and-down motion). Soothing fussy babies usually requires motion in all three planes. Experienced baby comforters have recognized this and developed a dance which goes something like this: With the baby in a sling or baby carrier, draped over your shoulder, or swaddled or nestled in your arms, you begin to walk, swaying from side to side (thus stimulating the side-to-side portion of the baby's vestibular system). After every few steps you bend back and forth, balancing on one foot while swinging the other foot forward. The third part of this little dance is the up-and-down motions, accomplished most easily with a heel-toe type of walk. You spring upward on the ball of your foot just until you feel a little bit of pulling in your calf muscles. It is more appropriate for a mother to say that she "dances with her baby" to comfort her rather than to say simply that she walks with the baby. This dance causes all three areas of the baby's vestibular system to be stimulated.

Research has shown that most infants are soothed best by the up-and-down motion of the dance. Some babies with aver-

Interesting sights and sounds can be calming for a fussy baby.

age levels of soothability are calmed simply by being carried in the parent's arms and walked with; that is the level of motion the unborn baby has been most accustomed to. The side-to-side swaying action is more natural for most parents than the up-and-down and back-and-forth movements. This is why you will very often see an experienced mother or father standing with feet planted on the ground but the rest of the body swaying from side to side while holding a sleeping baby. He or she is hoping that the motion will keep the baby asleep, especially at certain events where being a baby, let alone a crying baby, is not socially acceptable. In fact, parents do so much moving around during the first few months after birth that swaying back and forth becomes a way of life. A mother told me how she had been standing at a party holding a glass of ginger ale, when another mother came up and commented on the fact that she seemed to be teetering back and forth a bit. This observer then exclaimed, "I know you haven't had too much to drink, so I guess you must have just had a new baby."

Nursing on the move. A very effective soothing technique is to feed your baby while standing and swaying rhythmically from side to side or while rocking in a chair.

Baby's favorite dancing partner. Ever wonder why in some cases only the mother can soothe the baby? High-need babies are highly selective. Oftentimes only the mother can develop the proper soothing dance because she's the person who has been in motion with the baby for the previous nine months. It's as if the baby says to the mother, "I like your style." This also explains the frustration that some fathers discover when they try to give their wives some relief by trying to calm a fussy baby. The father's dance with the flailing, upset baby ends after a few minutes with "Here, you take her. I give up."

Fathers, take heart. Your baby is not rejecting you; she just hasn't grown accustomed to your style. The two of you haven't been dancing together for nine months, the way a mother and baby have. There will be times when an upset baby prefers a father's calm firm arms to the mother's tense ones which are tired out after a whole day of coping.

Speed. How fast to rock? Studies have shown that babies are soothed more easily by rocking done at a frequency of sixty to seventy cycles per minute. Isn't it interesting that this corresponds to the average rate of a mother's heartbeat and the average rhythm of walking? This further supports the concept that an infant is calmed best by duplicating the sound and motion she became accustomed to in the womb.

When the "womb" wears out

Soothing your baby with motions means you have to create the feeling that she is back in the womb. However, sooner or later your arms and legs get tired and the "womb" wears out. The following are some helpful hints that will keep the womb feeling going, even if mother or father is getting tired.

Slings. "Wearing" your baby is a highly effective strategy for calming the fussy baby. When you use a baby sling or other type of carrier to keep baby close to you, baby gets all the benefits of your presence and you have your hands free. Your hips and shoulders share in supporting baby's weight, so the sling brings relief when mother or father's arms are ready to give out from

Snuggle hold

Caring for an
Older Child

Cradle Hold

Kangaroo Hold

Snuggle Hold

Cradle hold

Hip Straddle

Hip Straddle

Snuggle Hold

hours of holding baby. If you are blessed with a high-need baby you'll find it helpful simply to get used to "wearing" your baby.

In our family, we have found that sling-type carriers are especially versatile and effective. The fabric of the sling encloses the baby, helping her keep her arms and legs under control. Baby is close to mother's heartbeat and the warmth of her body. She hears the familiar voice and enjoys the familiar motion. As babies mature and become more interested in the world around them, the sling provides a secure perch from which to look at ever-changing sights—much more interesting than lying in a crib looking at a mobile.

The key to making baby-wearing work for you is to make it part of your everyday lifestyle. Don't wait for your baby to fuss before you put her in the sling. Babies who are carried more fuss less. Make the sling your baby's special place whether she's happy and alert or tired and cranky. She will get used to feeling calm and peaceful while she's in the sling, and you will be able to get some chores done, play with an older child, or go out for a relaxing walk. Slings are useful when you are grocery shopping or doing errands with baby. Being close to you helps her feel secure, even in the over-stimulating environment of a supermarket or department store. And she will have a good view of all the interesting displays placed at the eye level of adults.

The sling is a great bedtime tool, especially for dads. After the baby has been fed, put her in the sling and take a gentle walk through the house or outdoors. You can even stand at your desk and read mail or watch the football game, as long as you keep moving a bit. Baby will soon fall asleep—but don't put her down just yet. Let her sleep in the sling, close to you, for twenty or thirty minutes, until you are certain she is sound asleep. Then go to the bed and lower baby and sling onto the mattress. Go slowly, especially if baby shows signs of waking up. Once baby has settled on the bed, slip the sling over your head and you can escape (or hang around and take a nap). You've helped baby make that important gradual transition from wakefulness to sleep.

Unlike most other baby carriers, slings can be used a variety of ways at different stages of a baby's development. Tiny infants nestle inside, older infants sit up in the front-facing position. When baby is big enough to ride your hip, the sling supports her weight and frees your hands for other tasks. Even fussy toddlers benefit from sling time.

For the best results, get your baby used to being in the sling in the first weeks of life. If you are feeling unsure of your sling skills, get some help from a veteran babywearer. Many La Leche League Groups sell baby slings, and LLL Leaders and members can help you learn to use one. One valuable tip we've passed on to many new mothers we've taught to use slings: after you put your baby in the sling, start walking immediately. The motion will help your baby settle in this new position. When she's older, she'll start to calm down or make eager noises just seeing you get ready to put her in the sling.

Other motion sources

Swings. Placing a fussy baby in a mechanical swing will often calm her and give parents a few minutes of much needed rest. These devices are usually set to swing at around sixty beats per minute. Fancier models may even provide an accompanying lullaby.

Some babies will not settle in swings. The reason is that most swings provide motion in only two planes, back and forth and slightly up and down. Some high-need babies are so selective that they will not calm down unless that third motion of swaying from side to side is added. This may be why being held and carried by an adult works better for calming babies than commercial swings. Mother or father can custom-tailor their motion to baby's preferences. Plus, there's a human being attached to this "swing."

Car rides. One successful technique for calming fussy babies and inducing sleep is what I call freeway therapy. Place baby in an approved car seat and take a ride. Rides on the freeway are the most effective; stopping and starting may awaken a sensitive baby who needs continuous monotonous movement. This technique is also called freeway fathering because it is particularly useful for fathers who want to give mother a break but discover that the baby will not settle dancing in dad's arms. This car ride can also be a family time because the two parents may have some uninterrupted conversation after the baby falls asleep. Driving for at least twenty minutes after the baby nods off allows her to enter the phase of deep sleep. You can then return home and pick up baby in the car seat and take her inside your home to finish her nap. If even this wakes her up and you, too, are desperate for sleep, stretch out in the car yourself and have a nap. Keep a pillow (or a novel) in the car just in case.

Trampolines. A father of a high-need baby told me that he is able to calm his baby by dancing rhythmically on a small home trampoline. This certainly makes sense in light of babies' need for stimulation in all three planes of motion. Dancing on a trampoline would allow dad to exaggerate the up-and-down, back-and-forth, and side-to-side movements. Chalk up another one for creative parents.

Baby carriages. Get an old-fashioned tub-like carriage with lots of springs, the type called a pram that bounces a lot. Gentle bouncing in these well-padded prams often works much better in soothing the baby than the new, collapsible, springless baby carriages. If you use a stroller, select one in which baby faces you.

Moving attractions. Things that move rhythmically and have a consistent, monotonous sound often soothe a fussy baby:
- Revolving ceiling fan
- Shower (place baby in an infant seat in the bathroom while you take a shower)
- Waves on a beach or a water fountain in your home

- Moving lights, such as a lava lamp or holiday decorations
- The pendulum of a clock
- Trees moving in the wind (place baby in front of a window to gaze at them).

Physical Contact: Getting in Touch with Your Baby

Holding your baby close to you is an effective soothing technique. Babies want to feel close to somebody, with as much skin-to-skin contact as possible.

A warm bath together

Fill the tub at least half full. Mother lies down in the tub holding the baby (or dad can hand the baby to her). Let baby half float while nursing, your breasts being just a few inches above the water line. Leave the faucet running and the tub's drain open just a bit. This not only provides the soothing sound of running water; it also keeps the water at a comfortable temperature (around 100 degrees Fahrenheit).

A warm fuzzy

Drape the bare-skinned but diapered baby over daddy's bare chest. Place baby's ear over daddy's heartbeat. Dad's heartbeat combined with the rhythm of his breathing movements along with firm rhythmic patting on the baby's back will usually soothe both members of this couple to sleep. In my experience, the warm fuzzy works best in the first three months; older babies squirm too much to lie quietly on dad's chest.

Dad should lie on the floor or on a bed when trying the "warm fuzzy." Don't try this on a sofa. If dad falls sleep and baby slides off his chest, baby may become wedged between her father's body and the cushions, which can cause suffocation. Beds should be pushed against the wall or have side rails if dad is sharing a nap with baby.

Baby can be soothed on dad's chest listening to his breathing and heartbeat.

Body massage

Massaging your baby will help her relax and calm down. Several books, including Dr. Frederick Leboyer's *Loving Hands* or Vimala McClure's *Infant Massage,* give instructions for massaging your baby. Chapter 5 has more information on baby massage.

Nestle nursing

When baby is tired, lie down together in bed or on the floor and curl up womblike around your baby, letting her snuggle close to your breasts, held in your arms, with as much skin-to-skin contact as possible. You can both nurse off to sleep this way.

Lambskin

Lambskin mats have been effective at soothing some babies. Lambskins have been specially shorn to be both safe and comfortable for babies and machine washable. Drape the lambskin on the bed or floor, and place baby on her back on the lambskin. The combination of the touch of the lambskin, the patting of your hand, and your closeness may soothe baby off to sleep.

Bending your baby

Some high-need babies tend to stiffen their muscles and arch their backs. They are difficult to hold because they don't cuddle easily. You can relax this kind of baby by carrying her in a bent forward position. When you bend your baby at the hips, she tends to relax her entire back, becoming less of an "archer," especially during feedings. Pumping baby's legs ("bicycling") may also help. Draping baby over a beach ball is another way to untense her. Many babies think this is fun.

Bending baby at the hips can help release gas or a stubborn bowel movement.

You can use your baby sling to help you hold baby in a bent position. The sling naturally cradles a reclining baby in a curved forward position. Slings are helpful for keeping babies who like to arch their backs in a good position at the breast during feedings. Babies old enough to support their own head and shoulders may enjoy sitting cross-legged in the sling, bent at the hips and facing forward.

Sounds That Soothe

Another group of gentling techniques uses various calming sounds to soothe the fussy baby. While some of the following suggestions may seem a bit unusual, they do work. Remember that babies are accustomed to sounds at a tempo resembling heartbeats, between sixty and seventy beats per minute, so if you can adjust the speed of the sound, do so. Here are some suggestions for soothing sounds:

Music may be soothing for a fussy baby.

- A metronome
- A ticking clock (turn the chimes off)
- Recordings of adult heartbeats and other womb sounds
- Running water from a faucet or shower
- The whirring hum of the vacuum cleaner, air conditioner, fan, dishwasher
- Recordings of ocean waves, waterfalls, rainfall, and other sounds from nature
- Mother or father singing lullabies, live or on tape (the lower, more monotonous, and more rhythmical the tone, the more soothing)
- Tape recordings of baby's own cry (played during crying episodes, these can startle a baby into silence, giving you a chance to apply other comforting measures)
- Calming classical music, for example, Mozart, Vivaldi, classical guitar, flute.

"White noise" works best to lull babies to sleep. This is the type of noise that is repetitive and monotonous and involves all the frequencies audible to the human ear. It has no message and lulls the mind into oblivion. Once you have found which types of white noise soothe your baby, make tape recordings of these sounds and play them on a tape recorder that has a continuous playback. One mother I know went through several vacuum cleaners before she realized that she could accomplish the same result by tape recording the vacuum cleaner sound.

You'll discover more methods of soothing your particular fussy baby. One mother of a high-need baby who was becoming desperate in her search for a way to quiet her baby shared the following unusual and ingenious technique with me. She strapped her baby into a car seat and strapped the seat on top of the washing machine while it was running. The humming and whirring vibrations of the machine lulled the baby to sleep. Perhaps automatic washing machines ought to include a cycle called "wash and sleep." (For safety's sake, the mother did not leave her baby alone on top of the washer.)

Sounds that soothe, dances that delight, and cuddles that comfort are all creative gentling techniques that bring out the best in parents and baby.

CHAPTER SEVEN

Feeding the Fussy Baby

During the first few months you will probably spend more time feeding your baby than in any other mother-baby interaction. Fussy babies, however, tend to be fussy feeders, and this can make feeding time difficult. This chapter will help you enjoy your baby's feeding times by making them easier for both of you.

Breast or Bottle: Does It Make a Difference?

Breastfeeding is clearly better for babies, especially fussy ones, and for their mothers. Breastfed babies are healthier, they have fewer respiratory and gastrointestinal infections, and they enjoy significant advantages in development. For mothers of high-need babies, breastfeeding can be a lifesaver, the most dependable comforting technique they have. Breastfeeding, after all, is designed to help both mother and baby feel better.

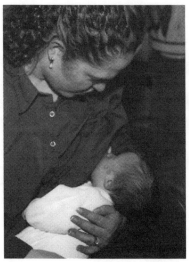

Breastfeeding has a calming effect on both mother and baby.

Special advantages for fussy babies

Fewer allergies. Breastfeeding eliminates the possibility of milk allergy, one cause of fussing and colic in babies. Some babies are allergic to the proteins in cow's milk or soy-based infant formula. Cow's milk proteins may cause allergic reactions and an overall unwell feeling.

More contact with mother. Because human milk is digested more rapidly than formula, breastfed babies need to be fed more often. This means they also get held more often. Fussy babies usually need more holding, and the breastfeeding relationship naturally provides them with extra skin-to-skin contact.

What's in it for mother?

Breastfeeding really pays off for mothers of fussy babies. A mother may be tempted to consider breastfeeding a fussy baby as too draining or too demanding. Many people overlook the fact that breastfeeding actually does something for the mother. Mothers of fussy babies feel that they are constantly giving to the baby, but a breastfeeding baby gives something back to the mother.

Breastfeeding increases the mother's level of prolactin, the "perseverance hormone." This hormone gives the mother an added boost during stressful times. Many mothers report that breastfeeding has a calming effect on themselves as well as their babies. Hormonal changes are probably responsible for this tranquilizing effect in the mother. There may also be substances in human milk that have not yet been identified which have a de-stressing effect on the baby. Researchers have found a sleep-inducing protein in mother's milk. Sitting down to breastfeed her baby forces a mother to relax. It forces her to put aside other obligations.

A breastfeeding mother can seldom ignore her baby. Breastfeeding mothers often show a greater sensitivity to their babies' signals. Breastfeeding is an exercise in baby-reading. Mothers learn to read baby's hunger cues and can respond to them promptly, without a trip to the kitchen to warm a bottle. Breastfeeding allows baby to be the only one in charge of how much he eats and how quickly, and as a mother learns to respect baby's "I'm done" signals, she also learns to trust that baby really does know what he needs. It may take nothing more than the baby's cry, or even a more subtle signal for hunger, to activate a mother's milk ejection reflex; her body reminds her that the baby needs her. Bottle-feeding mothers can also learn to read their babies well, but it takes more conscious effort without the physiological mechanisms that reinforce mothering in the lactating woman.

Substances in Mother's Milk That May Cause Fussiness

Although breastfeeding itself has a soothing effect on high-need babies, substances from the mother's diet that enter her milk may cause some babies to fuss. Small amounts of cow's milk protein can pass into a mother's milk and cause allergic reactions in some sensitive babies. Some mothers find that only large amounts of milk will affect the baby and that they can eat milk products such as yogurt and cottage cheese without any effect on the baby. Other babies may be bothered by any amount of milk or milk product in the mother's diet. If you think that something in your milk might be affecting your baby, try avoiding all milk products for two weeks and see if your infant's colic symptoms decrease or disappear. Keep a careful record of what you eat and of your baby's fussy spells to help you determine if there is a connection. Then reintroduce milk into your diet to see if symptoms reappear. If you're uncertain of the results, repeat the challenge test a second time. If your baby's symptoms recur, he is probably sensitive to cow's milk proteins, and you would be wise to avoid cow's milk while you are nursing him. Other common allergens in mother's diet include eggs, wheat, corn, nuts, and peanut butter.

Caffeine-containing substances in your diet may also bother your baby. These include coffee, tea, chocolate, colas, and some other soft drinks. Many over-the-counter medications also contain caffeine; check the label carefully if you or your baby is caffeine-sensitive. You may find that your baby's fussiness is tied to your caffeine intake. The occasional cup of coffee or that critical cup in the morning may not bother him, but coffee or cola all day long leads to a baby who won't settle down to sleep at night.

Gassy foods (for example, raw cabbage, onions, cauliflower,

green peppers, and broccoli) have also been implicated in colic. It is difficult to explain scientifically how gassy foods in the mother's diet cause gas in the baby, but who am I to argue with experienced mothers who claim this actually does happen?

On the whole, foods that breastfeeding mothers eat seldom bother most babies. If you're accustomed to tasting your milk, you may be able to detect when it takes on a different taste or smell. This can

Baby should be well supported so she can latch on effectively.

be a clue to understanding what's going on if your baby suddenly refuses the breast. Decongestants, caffeine-containing cold tablets, and prenatal vitamins taken by mother have also been known to cause fussiness in sensitive babies.

Breastfeeding Difficulties

It is important to correct breastfeeding difficulties early, especially in high-need babies. Breastfeeding is one

The football hold works well for some fussy babies.

of a mother's most reliable comforting measures. It is important that you and your baby get it working right. Babies who have difficulty breastfeeding may develop an unhealthy attitude toward nursing. The baby becomes programmed to fuss as soon as you start to nurse. A Leche League Leader or a trained lactation specialist can help you correct these difficulties early in your baby's life.

Positioning the fussy baby

"It's just the nature of the little beast," a mother lamented humorously as she tried to hang on to her squirming, arching, fussy baby who was pulling away from the breast. Fussy babies are not noted for their mealtime manners. They're inclined to throw their heads backwards and arch their backs; this can make breastfeeding difficult. When a baby arches his back and retracts his head, he throws his entire sucking mechanism out of alignment. His tongue falls into the back of his mouth, and he is unable to latch on to the breast correctly to get enough milk. Incorrect positioning of the baby at the breast can cause sore nipples and can also decrease the amount of stimulation the breasts receive. This in turn decreases the mother's milk supply.

These little "archers" need to be bent into a position that allows them to latch on properly. You can nurse the baby in the classic madonna or cradle position, supported by pillows in your lap, but his torso should be bent around your abdomen by firm pressure from your hand on his buttocks and thighs. The football hold also works well with babies who arch away from the breast. Baby is held under mother's arm on the same side he is feeding from, bent at the hips with the buttocks and legs up against the back of the chair; mother's hand has firm control of the baby's head, supporting it at the back of the neck. Bending your baby competes with and overrides his tendency to tense his muscles and arch his body. Using a baby sling during breast-feeding sessions can help you keep baby in a more relaxed, bent position.

Some babies arch away from the breast because of gastro-esophageal reflux (see page 80). They have learned to associate eating with pain and do not take the breast easily. It is important to investigate reasons for arching even while you teach your baby not to do it.

Besides a tendency to stiffen and arch, some hypertonic babies have a tendency to clench down hard on the breast, or their lip muscles are so tight and pursed that they cannot open their mouths wide and properly latch on to the areola. This can play havoc with tender nipples. Massaging the lip muscles before a feeding may get them to relax. Gently pressing down on your baby's chin with one of your fingers during feeding may also help him open his mouth wide, latch on, and nurse correctly.

If your fussy baby presents you with breastfeeding challenges right from the beginning, don't wait to get help. A La Leche League Leader can give you information and support and direct you to further resources in your community if you need them.

Sheltered nursing

Another problem with high-need babies that affects breastfeeding is that they may be hypersensitive and easily distractible. I call this kind of baby "Mr. Suck-a-Little, Look-a-Little." He goes on and off the breast several times during a feeding to have a look at all the enticing visual delights of his environment. This baby may need to be nursed in a dark quiet place, a practice called sheltered nursing.

Marathon nursing

"The baby wants to nurse all the time, day and night," complains a tired mother. High-need babies tend to go in for nursing marathons (as do all babies occasionally). They associate breastfeeding with more than just nourishment; they like the whole atmosphere of the restaurant. High-need babies seem particularly comfortable in the nursing position and quickly learn that breastfeeding is the number one comfort measure that helps them fit into their new environment. The closeness with mother, the rhythmic sucking, and the warm, sweet milk all help a stressed-out baby feel better. I frequently remind parents that "babies are takers and mothers are givers." Marathon nursing asks a lot of a mother, but it is one of the most important and effective techniques for mellowing a fussy baby. Like so many other parenting investments, if you can cope with these marathon periods, every ounce of your giving will return to you when your high-need baby becomes a giving child who feels right.

Improving your serve

Some fussy babies become very impatient if your milk is not served quickly enough. High-need babies often nurse greedily, and if not immediately satisfied, they may arch back and pull away from the nipple rather than persevere until the milk flows freely. A slow milk ejection reflex (also called a let-down) may account for some feeding fussiness in these impatient babies.

The following suggestions will help speed up your milk ejection reflex:

- Create a nursing station, a calm quiet area with a comfortable chair and pillows, perhaps some pleasant music, and a table to hold snacks and drinks, diapers, burping cloths, something for you to read, and things to entertain an older sibling. Take the phone off the hook.
- Take a warm shower or bath before nursing.
- Groom and caress the baby before nursing.
- Think milk. Imagine your body at work producing milk, like a fountain or stream.
- Position baby properly.
- Massage your breasts before nursing or use a pump or manual expression to get the milk flowing before the baby latches on.

Foremilk/hindmilk imbalance

The first milk a baby receives in a breastfeeding session is the milk that has been stored in the milk sinuses underneath the nipple. This milk, called the foremilk, is low in fat and high in lactose, the main carbohydrate in milk. As the baby's sucking activates the mother's milk ejection reflex, milk is squeezed out of the milk-making cells higher up in the mother's breast and sent down towards the nipple. This hindmilk is higher in fat. The fat level in milk rises during the feeding, and the high fat levels later in the feeding bring baby the calories he needs to grow. They may also signal him to slow down and feel full.

Sometimes babies get too much of the foremilk and not enough of the hindmilk, and this can cause fussiness. The baby may not be able to digest all the lactose easily and he gets gas pains. He may also have watery, explosive greenish stools and a sore red rash around the anus. This is especially likely to happen in a baby who feeds quickly or who is switched to the second breast after only a few minutes on the first side. He may get enough of the foremilk to supply the calories he needs, but his system is overloaded with lactose. This can also happen to a baby whose mother has an oversupply of milk.

This is why breastfeeding experts advise mothers to "finish the first breast first." Offer the other side only when baby seems satisfied after actively nursing at the first breast and deciding to come off on his own. This will allow baby to get more calories from hindmilk rather than getting bloated on the foremilk.

Overfeeding

Some babies may fuss because their tummies are too full. Some mothers have especially strong milk-ejection reflexes, which flood the baby with milk.

If an over-abundant supply of milk seems to be part of the problem, try offering just one breast at a feeding. If baby wants to nurse again within an hour or two, offer the "empty" breast from the last feeding. The high-fat milk still present there will satisfy baby. Then offer the other breast at the next feeding.

Less milk fed more often will help baby feel more comfortable. Since levels of fat in milk decline as the time between feedings increases, baby will get more of the calories he needs if you nurse him more frequently. His stomach will be more comfortable handling a lower volume of milk fed to him every hour or two. Babies' tiny stomachs are not designed to digest giant meals.

Swallowing air at the breast

Breastfed babies tend to swallow less air while feeding than bottle-fed babies. This is because they have more control over the whole feeding process. Studies have shown that bottle-feeding is physiologically stressful for infants when compared to breastfeeding. Babies at the breast show a more regular rhythm for sucking, swallowing, and breathing.

Some mothers do have stronger milk-ejection reflexes than others, and some babies are better than others at coping with a torrent of milk. Babies who have to gulp and struggle to keep up may fuss and struggle at the breast. A fast milk flow can also cause them to swallow air, which leads to intestinal discomfort after the feeding. This problem may be related to the oversupply problem mentioned above. An oversupply of milk combined with the force of gravity can produce a strong let-down reflex. Nursing on only one breast at each feeding can help bring the supply in line with baby's needs and make the milk flow more manageable. Manually expressing a little milk prior to feeding can decrease the force of the let-down and make it easier for the baby to nurse.

Babies who are not latched on well and don't have a good seal on the breast may also tend to swallow air during feedings. A baby who comes off the breast easily—without you having to break the suction—probably doesn't have a good seal and may swallow air. Clicking sounds while sucking are another sign of a poor seal. Careful attention to how the baby latches on can correct this.

Engorged, distended breasts make it hard for baby to latch on and form a good seal on the areola. Engorgement flattens out the nipple and areola (the pigmented area around the nipple). Consequently the baby sucks only on the nipple instead of getting part or all of the areola into his mouth. He doesn't get enough milk this way, but he does swallow a lot of air. When he cries and protests about his difficulties, he may swallow even more air. You can minimize problems with engorgement right from the start by not limiting your baby's access to the breast. Encourage him to nurse frequently and long enough to empty the breasts. Warm compresses and manual expression will release some milk before feedings, softening the areola and making it easier for baby to nurse correctly.

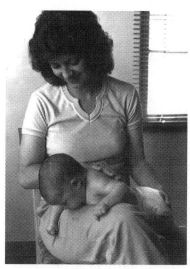

Lay baby on your lap and pat his back to bring up a burp.

When the Fussy Baby Is Formula-Fed

"We've tried so hard to find the right formula," complained a frantic couple as they ran down their checklist of everything they'd tried to calm their fussy baby. In my experience, formula changes are way down on the list of things that work for colicky babies. Just to do something, parents may go from doctor to doctor, each of whom will suggest one formula after another. By the time the parents have tried all the formulas available on the supermarket shelf, the baby outgrows the colic, but the doctor who made the last suggestion gets credit for finally having found the right formula. Some colicky babies are helped by a change from cow's milk formula to one made with soy, although some babies who are allergic to cow's milk formulas will also be allergic to soy formulas. Some colicky babies improve when switched to a predigested formula. They are expensive and not very appealing. Consult your doctor if you are not breastfeeding and need to choose a formula for your baby.

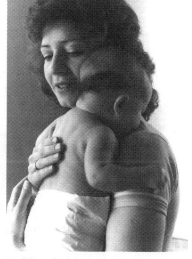

Holding baby upright after feedings may avoid spit-ups.

Feeding and Burping Positions

Fussy feeders tend to spit up frequently; regurgitation is one of the calling cards of a colicky baby, whether breast- or bottle-fed. Air-swallowers spit up because a trapped bubble of air settles underneath food in the stomach. When the stomach contracts, it pushes the air against the food, and like a pneumatic pump, the air forcefully expels whatever is in the way.

If you have a colicky baby, be prepared to go through many shoulder burp rags during the first six months. Regurgitation subsides markedly when baby begins to spend most of his day in the upright position. The amount the baby spits up always seems like more than it really is. If your baby is gaining weight, growing in height, and generally thriving, spitting up is most likely a temporary nuisance rather than a sign of an underlying medical problem. Babies who swallow a lot of air also tend to be frequent feeders. Once the swallowed air is removed, the stomach feels empty and signals the need for another feeding.

The art of feeding the colicky baby lies in allowing the least amount of air to get in and getting the most air back up. Success at "winding" the baby was, in grandmother's day, the badge of an experienced baby feeder. Keeping the baby upright during feeding minimizes air swallowing and makes it easier to bring up the air later. Hold the baby at a thirty degree or greater angle throughout the feeding. This allows the air to settle at the top of the stomach where it can be more easily burped

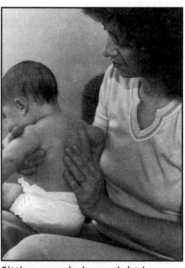

Sitting your baby upright in your lap and patting him gently on the back is a good way to bring up a burp.

out before it has a chance to make its way down through the intestines and cause colic pains. (This upright position also helps a baby cope with the fast flow of milk that accompanies a strong milk-ejection reflex.) Following the feeding, keep baby upright at a ninety-degree angle for at least twenty minutes. You can sit him on your lap, drape him over your shoulder in a rocking chair, or stand up and sway back and forth rhythmically. Avoid jostling the baby after feeding or you're liable to be punished with a shot of partially digested food all over your shirt.

The most effective burping position is one where baby is sitting upright on your knee or lap, slightly bent forward against your hand which supports the middle of his abdomen. Gently pat his back with your other hand. Some babies are difficult to burp, and some babies seldom need to be burped. If you don't hear a burp within ten minutes, further efforts to get out the elusive trapped air bubbles will probably go unrewarded.

Overeating and the Fussy Baby

Some high-need babies overeat but don't "overgrow," others overeat and "overgrow." This may be another reason for the importance of breastfeeding. Early on, high-need babies associate feeding with comfort, and this is why they tend to feed often and for long stretches at a time. This is where there is an exciting difference between breastfeeding and bottle-feeding. The baby does not always get the same kind of milk at the breast. When he nurses just a little bit for comfort or as a "pick-me-up" during a stressful time, he receives the lower calorie foremilk. When he nurses for a longer time to satisfy his hunger he also gets the creamier, high-calorie hindmilk. A bottle-fed baby, on the other hand, gets the same high-calorie formula whether he nurses for hunger or for comfort. If bottle-fed babies fed as often as breastfed babies do, they would all be little blimps. Breastfed babies, on the other hand, may be less at risk for obesity in later childhood and adolescence. New studies support this observation.

The need for frequent feedings may explain the tendency to introduce solids earlier in bottle-fed fussy babies. Bottle-feeding mothers are required to come up with creative ways to comfort their babies since they cannot feed them as often as breastfeeding mothers.

The baby's body type has a lot to do with his growth, especially if he is a frequent feeder. High-need babies with an ectomorph body type (slender and bony) may eat incessantly but burn off a lot of energy and remain lean. Infants with mesomorph or endomorph body types (short with pudgy hands and feet and squat large bones) are the ones who grow plump when they overeat. Many babies who are plump by their six-month birthdays use up this stored energy when they begin to crawl, walk, and run.

Starting Solid Foods in the Fussy Baby

"It's about time you fed that baby something," said the well-meaning grandmother to her daughter who sat breastfeeding her baby for the third time in the last three hours; the obviously well-nourished infant was already at the top of her class on the growth chart.

Introducing solid foods has long been touted as a panacea for whatever ails the tiny baby. The generation of parents who bottle-fed their infants has not completely come to grips with the biologic fact that their grandchildren can grow quite well on nothing but their mothers' milk for the better part of the first year. Introducing solid foods too early (before the middle of the first year) may aggravate colic; at best it has little effect on babies' behavior and seldom helps them sleep through the night. Since colicky babies have a slightly increased risk of developing allergies, I advise parents to wait with solid foods until the baby's development shows readiness, rather than going by the calendar. Signs that the baby is ready for solid foods include:

- Baby sits well without support.
- Baby can pick up small objects with his thumb and forefinger.
- Baby has been marathon nursing for more than a week, but still doesn't seem satisfied.

The presence or absence of teeth doesn't affect your baby's readiness or ability to handle solid food. His grabbing at your food does not necessarily mean he's ready for solids either; by the time he is four or five months old, he will be grabbing for everything in sight, especially anything that mother seems to be interested in.

A mashed-up very ripe banana is a good starting food because its sweet taste is very similar to mother's milk. Place a small amount of banana on the tip of your baby's tongue as a test. If the banana goes in, he's ready; if the banana comes right back at you, he's not ready. Unfortunately the most popular first foods for babies, rice cereal and bananas, are also constipating. The last thing a colicky baby needs is constipation. If you notice that your baby's stools are getting harder after starting solid foods, back off before he gets plugged up. Colicky babies who are allergic to cow's milk also have a higher incidence of being allergic to other foods such as citrus, tomatoes, and berries. It would be wise to introduce new solid foods very gradually in these babies.

Introducing solid foods too early may be particularly detrimental to high-need babies. When solid foods are used as a substitute for rather than a complement to breastfeeding, the frequency of feedings decreases. The mother's milk supply diminishes, and baby may find breastfeeding less satisfying and less comforting. The baby who becomes fussier following the early introduction of solid foods may be expressing his unhappiness about decreased chances to breastfeed and his mother's low milk supply. Besides causing fussiness, introducing solid foods too early may reduce mother's coping ability. Frequent nursing keeps a mother's prolactin levels high. Babies nurse less frequently when they begin to eat substantial portions of solid foods. Both members of the nursing pair lose by too early an introduction to solid foods.

Junk foods and fussy babies

Highly sugared foods and those with artificial colors and flavors should be avoided in all babies, but particularly in fussy babies. High-need babies often grow up to be high-need children, and high-need children seem to be particularly vulnerable to behavioral changes caused by junk food. Inevitably, children encounter junk food in social situations, but if they are not given junk food during the first few years, they become more aware of its effects. They are more likely to realize that they don't feel right and don't act right after eating junk food. This is a sort of reverse addiction. When a baby grows up learning to feel right after feedings, he won't like the feeling he gets after eating junk food as an older child. He'll be more likely to turn down junk food.

Weaning the High-Need Baby

"What! You're still nursing," said the shocked relatives to the mother who was breastfeeding her two-year-old high-need baby. These babies not only have a high level of need, but the needs also last longer.

Tired mothers may ask, "How long?" I have a little sign in my office which says, "Early weaning not recommended for babies." I'd like to add here, "Especially not for high-need babies." The timing of weaning is critical, and understanding the real meaning of the term weaning will help you decide when and how you should wean your high-need child.

In ancient writings, weaning meant "to ripen." The word used when a fruit was ripe and ready to be picked from the vine was the same as the word used for weaning. Weaning was a positive step and wasn't associated with the end of a relationship. When a child was weaned, all the people of the tribe got together and celebrated, but not because the mother was finally free of the child. Weaning was a festive occasion because the child was now ripe and ready to take on new relationships such as the beginning of formal instruction by his father and the wise men in the town. A child was weaned from the security of his mother into the arms of the culture with no break in the action. (See, for example, Genesis 21:8, 1 Samuel 1:21-24.) The image of a weaned child was used to describe a state of peace and tranquillity in Psalm 131:

> I have stilled and quieted my soul,
> Like a weaned child with its mother,
> Like a weaned child is my soul within me.

Think of weaning as a time of fulfillment when the child feels so right and so ready that he looks up and says, "Thanks, Mom and Dad. I am filled with this relationship, and I am ready to take on other ways of connecting with parents and other significant persons."

Life is a series of weanings for a child: weaning from the womb, weaning from the breast, weaning from the parents' bed, weaning from home to school, from school to work. The age at which a child is ready to wean varies tremendously, especially among high-need children. A child who is weaned from any of these stages before he is ready is at high risk of developing what I call diseases of premature weaning: anger, aggression, mood swings, just plain not feeling right. Weaning too early is one of the common causes of delayed fussiness. A mother might say, "She was such an easy baby for the first eight months, and now she's a bear." Tantrum-like behavior is especially common after abrupt weaning.

When I want to know the hows and whys of a certain aspect of child development, I sit back and watch what a child does over time when parents guide and channel his behavior without frustrating it. Looking back over the high-need breastfed babies I have watched grow and develop, I would say that babies who are allowed unlimited access to mother usually wean sometime toward the end of the second year or later. Nap-time and bed-time nursings are usually the last ones to be given up. As a firm believer that babies do what they are designed to do, I would advise that mothers of high-need babies consider the duration of breastfeeding in terms of years and not months. Weaning should take place when both members of the nursing couple are willing and able to move on.

Remember that weaning means graduating from one stage of development to another. Keep in mind that in the continuum of parenting, high-need babies become high-need children. As children get older their needs don't decrease; they only change. When a child is weaned from the mother's breast, the parents' roles as creative designers of a child's environment become more important. High-need children are prone to becoming bored unless stimulated by an enriched environment that channels their minds into meaningful activities. Following weaning, be prepared for your high-need child to up the ante continually in the parenting game.

Be prepared to get a lot of flack about nursing your toddler. Well-meaning friends and relatives will not hesitate to tell you, "You're making him too dependent." This is a carry-over from the days when the effectiveness of a mother was judged by how soon her baby was eating three square meals a day, was sleeping through the night, and was completely weaned and toilet trained. Early independence was the goal. In my opinion, this is absolute nonsense. A baby, especially a high-need baby, must go through a normal period of dependence before he can comfort-ably handle independence. He must be emotionally filled before he can learn how to give; he must learn how to handle attach-ment before he can manage detachment. I want to leave moth-ers of those babies who seem destined to wean late with an encouraging thought: the most secure and independent children in my practice are those who have not been weaned before they were ready.

If you want to know more about nursing toddlers, or just plain need to meet other mothers who have "been there and done that," call a La Leche League Leader in your area. At meetings of your local La Leche League Group you'll find support for nursing your toddler, along with ideas for handling the challenges of mothering a high-need toddler.

CHAPTER EIGHT

Fathering the Fussy Baby

"I could not have done it without my husband," confided a mother after surviving the first year of parenting her high-need baby. In looking over the records of high-need babies in my practice who have had a good outcome, one parenting characteristic stands out above all the others: a consistently involved and supportive father.

This chapter explores many of the common feelings that fathers of fussy babies have shared with me. It will also help fathers understand why mothers of high-need babies act the way they do, as well as suggest ways in which fathers can make wise investments that can change fussy liabilities into creative assets.

Father Feelings and the Fussy Baby

"All my wife does is nurse."

"She's too attached to that baby."

Dads can take over when mother's arms are worn out.

"We've got to get away together. I have needs, too."
"She prefers to be with our baby rather than me."
"The baby just won't settle down for me. I feel helpless."
"We haven't made love for weeks."

These are real feelings from real fathers who sincerely love their wives and children. But they feel frustrated with their own inability to comfort their fussy babies, and they are confused about their wives' strong attachment to their babies.

Understanding and coping with these normal feelings requires an understanding of some basic concepts, especially the concept of levels of need. Your baby comes wired with a certain level of needs, and if these needs are filled, the baby fits well into her environment. This good fit has a positive effect on her temperament, and she feels right and brings joy to her parents. If the baby's needs are not filled, her temperament may be negatively affected because she feels that she does not fit into her environment. She is at high risk for not feeling right within herself and could become a trial to her parents. In other words, babies are born to take, and somebody has to give. Who's going to be the giver? Naturally the job of filling the needs of these high-need babies falls primarily on the mother. I say naturally for two reasons:

- The baby is more accustomed to the mother.
  After all, they have grown together for the last
  nine months.
- The mother is biologically and hormonally programmed to be sensitive to the needs of her
  baby, especially in the first two to three years.

This does not mean that fathers have nothing to do with baby care. But it just does not come as naturally for most fathers as it does for mothers. We have to work harder at it.

Babies have a way of extracting from their mothers the amount of energy required for filling their needs and helping them fit into their new environment. Mothers, in turn, are programmed to be giving and nurturing and to supply the energy demanded by the baby. This is nature's law of supply and demand that ensures the survival of the young of the species. But who fills the mother's needs? Father has to supply this missing ingredient.

In order for the parenting economic system to work, there are certain conditions that have to be met. These conditions prepare the mother for her job and help her grow and mature. They build up her stamina, her milk supply, her levels of mothering hormones, and her overall sensitivity to her baby. She not only can survive, but also thrive as the mother of a high-need baby. These conditions include:

- A positive birthing experience
- Continued mother-baby togetherness in the
  postpartum period
- Unrestricted breastfeeding
- Mother and baby sleeping close to each other,
  that is, sharing sleep

- Responding promptly to baby's cries
- Not weaning until the baby is ready.

These mothering practices may seem idealistic, but most, if not all of them, are necessary if you have a high-need baby. They really do build up a mother's ability to cope.

A new mother cannot be all things to all people. If she is blessed with a high-need baby, she has to reapportion her energies. The time and caring that were previously parceled out in appropriate amounts to the people around her are now directed primarily toward the baby. Other people feel left out, including her husband. During that short period of time when the baby is so totally dependent on the mother, this redirection of time, emotion, and energy is very necessary.

Sexual feelings

Fathers of high-need babies also feel confused at their wives' apparent lack of sexual interest. An understanding of the hormonal changes that go on in your wife after birth may help you to understand this temporary lack of sexual drive. Before the baby is born, a woman's sexual hormones have a greater effect on her behavior than her maternal hormones. After giving birth this changes, and the mothering hormones predominate. Providing the environment is supportive and the mother is willing and able, the mothering hormones will dominate the sexual hormones as long as this is necessary to fill the

Dads need to get involved early in learning their own special ways to comfort a fussy baby.

baby's needs. This doesn't mean that your wife has lost interest in you sexually; it just means that the energies which were previously directed toward you are temporarily redirected toward your baby. This is how the system was designed to function, especially with a high-need baby.

Everyone makes demands of the new mother, especially the baby. By bedtime, it is very normal for a mother to want to say, "Don't bother me. Just let me go to sleep." Overwhelmed by physical closeness to the baby and perhaps by the demands of another small child, mothers of high-need babies often tell me, "I feel all 'touched out' by the end of the day."

What Dads Can Do
Help at home

Provide your wife with some domestic help to free her from chores that drain her energy away from the baby. Help with the housework yourself, or if you can afford it, consider hiring someone to clean or do whatever needs to be done. In my experience, mothers of high-need babies don't get worn out so much by the baby alone. It's all the additional commitments that really do them in. Avoid putting pressure on your wife to be the perfect hostess, social chairman, entertainer, and housekeeper. This is also a time to accept the fact that your castle may never again be as tidy as it once was. Freeing a mother from other responsibilities is especially important when the baby is going through a particularly demanding period. If your baby is in one of those "all he wants to do is nurse" periods, be sure all mother has to do is nurse. Even though we as fathers cannot breastfeed our babies, we can create an environment that helps our wives nurse better.

Respect the mother's sensitivity to the baby's cries

Avoid offering the "let the baby cry it out" advice. Keep in mind that mothers are wired differently than fathers in regard to sensitivity to a baby's cries. A baby's cry sets up a physiologic change in the mother, but father experiences no such change. When and how to respond to a baby's cries is one case where mother certainly knows best.

Avoid pressuring the new mother

I've spent many hours counseling young mothers who feel that their husbands are pressuring them to go against their mothering instincts. These husbands are causing their wives to feel guilty about not being perfect wives and exciting companions. The most common expression of this kind of pressure is the "we need to get away" syndrome. Let me share with you a real situation which illustrates this point.

Dan and Susan were proud parents of a three-month-old high-need baby girl, Jessica. Susan was doing well at meeting Jessica's needs and having some energy left over for herself and her relationship with her husband. Both Jessica and Susan were thriving, but Dan was feeling left out. Dan had a chance to close a big business deal across the country and figured it was time that he and Susan got away together alone. He pressured Susan to leave Jessica behind (and wean her, too) so that the two of them could fly away and rekindle their romance. Dan also felt that Susan would be an asset in closing the deal.

In talking to both of them, I convinced Dan that he was putting Susan in a no-win situation. One side of her felt that yes, she would like to get away with Dan, but her deep maternal instincts told her that Jessica was not ready to be left alone. If they did leave her behind, the whole family would lose: Susan would not be the relaxed and romantic mate that Dan wanted with him on the trip, and Jessica would make them pay for this premature weaning when they got back.

The solution? Dan, Susan, and Jessica took off together for New York. (Jessica nursed all the way from coast to coast.) They were surprised to discover that Dan's business contact also had his wife and baby along. The wife exclaimed, "I'm so happy you

A father's support of breastfeeding helps it go more smoothly.

brought your baby along, too. We have one of those babies who just can't be left." The two fathers had an instant rapport because they had both bucked the same system and shown that their babies had top priority in their lives. The business deal was closed successfully.

I hope this explanation of normal maternal feelings will help fathers cope with their own feelings. You have not been displaced by your baby, but the energies that were previously directed toward you are now redirected toward your baby. This is a season of the marriage, a time to mother, a time to father. If you nurture your wife as she nurtures your baby, her energies will return to you and at such a high level of warmth and maturity that you will know that you have made a good investment.

The Care and Feeding of New Mothers

A new mother needs mothering, too. The most important ingredient in parenting the high-need baby—more important than breastfeeding, sleeping with the baby, responding to her cries—is a stable and fulfilling marriage. In order for the attachment style of parenting to work, it needs to be sheltered by the umbrella of the father loving and nurturing the mother as she nurtures their child. At this point you may be thinking, "I understand the system, but what can I do to help?" One father of a high-need newborn put it very well: "I can't always console our baby, but I can do everything possible to make it easier for my wife to console him."

Be involved early

Ideally a father's involvement with parenting begins during pregnancy. Attend prepared childbirth classes with your wife so that you can be present and involved in the birth of your baby. After the baby is born, pitch in and help. Change diapers, bathe the baby, wash dishes, cook, clean house, anything that can free up your wife to do what no one else can do—be a mother to your child. Some fathers may feel that domestic chores are not their job, but mothers' and fathers' roles are not so clearly defined as they were decades ago. Back then a mother was likely to be surrounded with an extended family which pitched in and took over domestic chores in the first weeks after the birth of a baby. Many young families today do not enjoy the luxury of living close to their extended families. In today's mobile society, father's role in the family needs to be extended.

Communicate your commitment

Sit down with your wife regularly and reaffirm your commitment to her as a husband and to your baby as a father. You might even read this chapter and discuss it together. In our family we have a custom that I call "inventory time." From time to time I sit down with my wife and simply ask her how she's doing. You may be surprised when your wife breaks down and confides, "I thought you'd never ask. I'm getting so burned out." She may have been working hard to keep up a good front while feeling overwhelmed and exhausted. Don't assume that all is well unless you hear otherwise. Ask.

Periodic "I care" messages give your wife the security that you are committed to this entire relationship. Impress upon her that you truly understand the concept of the high-need baby and reassure her that you are all in this together.

Tune in

A mother who was under a lot of stress because of the demands of her high-need baby once told me, "I'd have to hit my husband over the head before he'd realize that I'm giving out." Dads, while mothers are noted for their untiring energy in giving, they don't always know when their energy is giving out. They will continue to run a long time on an almost empty tank without calling for help. Be sensitive to the early warning signals of maternal burnout and come to the rescue early.

Gentling Tips for Fathers

It is very frustrating for dads when their babies don't respond to their comforting measures. Babies do have a preference for mother, but there are things that dads can do sometimes even better than mothers. See Chapter Five for more about gentling techniques such as warm fuzzies, freeway fathering, and colic dances. Here are some more tips especially for fathers on comforting fussy babies.

Sing to your baby

While it is true that most babies pay closer attention to the higher pitch of mother's voice, some babies are soothed more easily by low-pitched male voices. Sing humming, droning, rather monotonous songs such as "Old Man River."

Take over during high-need times

Babies don't time their fussy periods conveniently. They seem to fuss most in the late afternoon or early evening—a time which unfortunately coincides with father coming home. While fussy

Drifting Apart

Mary and Tom came into my office one day with anxious looks on their faces. Divorce seemed imminent. Mary related that she had been blessed with a high-need baby. She tried so hard to be a "good" mother: she took her baby with her everywhere, nursed on demand, slept with the baby, picked him up every time he cried, and was always at baby John's beck and call. Because Tom didn't know much about babies and crying babies scared him, Mary seldom released the baby into his care. This only reinforced Tom's feeling of inadequacy, and he sought consolation in longer hours at the office. As Mary got more and more into her mothering, Tom got more and more into his job; the two drifted further and further apart, and baby John kept fussing. Mary increased her attachment mothering, while Tom began forming some outside "attachments" of his own. Mary realized that she and Tom were not communicating but justified it by thinking, "My baby needs me. Tom is a big boy. He can take care of himself." Fortunately, this couple had the wisdom to realize that they were headed down the wrong road. They sought help and the situation had a happy ending.

Dr. Sears comments: *I include this real life story in order to urge couples to realize that healthy family dynamics must have balance. Mutual sensitivity keeps a two-parent family thriving and intact. This is vitally important in the parenting of a high-need child. I feel very strongly that a good marriage is necessary for parenting the high-need baby. Unfortunately, when mothers and fathers are not working together in parenting their high-need child, the marriage undergoes a lot of stress and strain.*

babies have better periods and worse periods during the course of a day, dads usually see more of the worse periods. This does absolutely nothing for the father-child relationship. More often it prompts the question, "Is he always like this?"

You can really make points with your tired wife by taking over during the fussy part of the day. This is the scenario: tired dad arrives home and is greeted by a tired mom and fussy baby. Instead of sitting down to relax and unwind from the day's tensions undisturbed, tired dad scoops up the fussy baby and waltzes him off for a car ride, a long walk, or maybe just a dance around the house, leaving the tired wife with the message, "You do something just for yourself." Try this, dads. You may surprise your wife so much that she may have a surprise or two in store for you when you return.

Mothers can help avoid some of this late afternoon fussing by putting babies down for naps later in the afternoon. Baby then awakens shortly before dad arrives home, and he at least is not greeted by a tired baby. This generally is a lot easier on the whole family than keeping the baby up in hopes that he'll fall asleep early in the evening so the adults can finally have some peace and quiet time together.

What's in It for You?

Dads, if you have been consistently involved in fathering your high-need baby and in nurturing your wife, you will profit. First of all, you will know your child better. By spending more time with your child, especially during those high-need periods, you will begin to see not only the difficult side of your child's temperament but also its strong points. There really are many.

You will also feel more adept as a father. Many fathers are unjustly portrayed as bumbling males who don't know how to change a diaper. This simply is not true. There is such a thing as father's intuition, but we males have to work at it harder. It takes longer to develop than mother's intuition.

Increasing your involvement with your high-need baby will also help your marriage prosper. One of the greatest ways that you can increase the respect your wife has for you is to care for her child. Your high-need child will bring out the best in you.

CHAPTER NINE

Nighttime Parenting of the High-Need Child

"Why do high-need babies need more of everything but sleep?" asked a tired mother. One of the "for better or for worse" aspects of nighttime parenting is that babies usually carry their daytime temperament into the night.

Some studies have shown that so-called easy babies go to sleep more easily and stay asleep longer than difficult babies (Sears 1999; Weissbluth and Liel 1983). In some studies, babies with more sensitive temperaments slept an average of two hours less at night and one hour less during the day. This is a paradox for tired parents. You would think that high-need babies would need more sleep; their parents do. One father aptly put it this way: "When it comes to sleep, I'm a high-need parent."

Why High-Need Babies Sleep Differently

High-need babies carry the temperamental traits of their waking personalities into the nighttime. Parents will often describe their special baby as "tiring but bright." This brightness is what keeps high-need babies awake. They seem to be constantly awake and aware. It's as if they were endowed with an internal light that is not easily turned off.

The stimulus barrier

Babies have a stimulus barrier which enables them to block out unpleasant stimuli. One of the ways that most babies block out environmental stimuli is by falling asleep. High-need babies have an immature stimulus barrier. Their sensory thresholds are lower; in other words, you do not have to bother them much in order to get a reaction. Hunger, discomfort, cold, and loneliness tend to awaken a high-need baby easily, even though a baby with a higher sensory threshold may sleep through these same disturbances. Part of high-need babies' increased sensitivity comes from being constantly aware of their environment. They are always tuned into and processing the delights of the world around them. Their radar systems don't shut down easily.

Sleep maturity

Another reason why high-need babies sleep less is that they take longer to develop sleep maturity. There are two general stages of sleep: light sleep and deep sleep. It is much easier to arouse an individual from light sleep than from deep sleep. Babies have a greater percentage of light sleep than adults do; this difference has both survival and developmental benefits. Also, as babies move from one sleep state to the next, they go through a transition period in which they are vulnerable to waking. As a baby grows older the amount of light sleep diminishes, the amount of deep sleep increases, and transitions are made more easily. Babies begin to sleep better.

High-need babies take longer to develop sleep maturity.

They seem to have longer and more frequent periods of light sleep. Consequently they are restless and squirming during a large part of the night. (I suspect that these babies also enjoy a more intense kind of deep sleep; they really seem "zonked" when they are in the deep sleep stage.) As periods of light sleep alternate with periods of deep sleep throughout the night, high-need babies seem to be more likely to wake up during vulnerable transition periods.

Sleep Survival Tips
Nursing down

It is totally unrealistic for parents of a high-need baby to put him down in a crib and expect to watch him settle himself into a deep slumber. It seldom works that way. These babies need to be "parented to sleep" rather than just put to bed. They need help shutting down.

A technique that has been successful in our family is what we call nursing down: rock your baby, walk with him, and nurse him as a before-bed ritual. What you are actually doing is gentling your baby into tuning out the distractions of his world and enticing him into the initial period of light sleep. You then continue nursing and rocking your baby in your arms until he appears to have drifted through the initial period of light sleep (approximately twenty minutes). He now enters the deep sleep state and will seem to melt into your arms. Now you can put him down.

If you try to get baby out of your arms and into bed too early, before he is fully into the deep sleep phase, he very likely will wake up and demand that you repeat the whole bedtime ritual. In fact, it probably will take longer the second time around. These babies are so ultrasensitive that a change of position or the change in the pull of gravity that accompanies being lowered into bed is enough to awaken them from light sleep. Experienced mothers frequently say, "The baby has to be fully

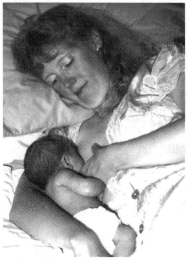

It's worth experimenting to find a comfortable position to nurse lying down.

asleep before I can put him down."

Dads can use the "nursing down" ritual, too, but instead of nursing the baby to sleep, they can "wear him down" in a baby sling. Once baby has settled into in a deep sleep by walking and swaying with dad, he can be transferred into bed easily by lowering the sling to the mattress and slipping it over your head.

Nestle nursing

In some ultrasensitive babies this rock-and-nurse ritual is not enough. They settle better if after the nursing down phase mother and baby simply curl up next to each other and nurse off to sleep. These bright little babies do not seem to want to change levels of consciousness (from awake to asleep) alone and need to fall asleep in the company of someone else.

The Advantages of Sharing Sleep

Where should the baby sleep? I usually tell parents that wherever all three of you get the most sleep is the right arrangement for your family. In my experience, most high-need babies sleep better when they sleep with their parents. (In fact, to most high-need babies, crib is a four-letter word.) Most parents sleep better this way, too. It is the nature of these sensitive babies to want harmony in their environment both by day and by night. Sleeping with your baby is often called "the family bed." I prefer to call this beautiful arrangement "sharing sleep." Babies share more than the physical space with their mothers; they also share sleep cycles.

Sharing sleep cycles

Sharing sleep helps mother and baby organize their sleep cycles. They sleep in harmony with each other. Mother and baby are close to each other when baby begins to stir and enter a vulnerable period for night-waking. Mother can then nurse the baby right through this vulnerable period of lighter sleep and help him re-enter the state of deep sleep while preventing his waking up completely. Mothers who begin this arrangement early enough (right after birth) usually find that their own light sleep stages coincide with their babies' sleep cycles. Mother's deep sleep is not interrupted, and she feels more rested.

Easier breastfeeding

With the sharing sleep arrangement it is not necessary for the baby to wake up crying in order to signal feeding time. If the baby wakes up hungry and alone, he must cry to summon his mother. If mother is not close by, he must cry even harder. By the time mother arrives both she and baby are fully awake, and it takes longer for both of them to get back to sleep after the feeding. In this instance, baby learns to cry harder; this works against your daytime efforts to mellow your high-need baby's temperament and teach him to cry better rather than harder.

Mothers who sleep with their babies may have higher prolactin levels because of the more frequent feeding. Thus they get an added hormonal boost to help them survive and thrive with their high-need babies. Babies who sleep with their mothers are also less likely to wean before they are ready.

Over the years I have advocated the sharing sleep arrangement in my books and in my pediatric practice, and we have enjoyed it in our own family. It is beautiful and it works! In general, I have noticed that babies who share sleep with their parents exude a feeling of rightness and security—the serenity of a child who is in harmony with his world by day and by night.

Coping with the All-Night Nurser

Even when sharing sleep, nighttime parenting can take its toll, especially on parents who are wakened frequently for months by a high-need baby. They wonder, "Will this baby ever learn to sleep?" Here are some tips that can help you minimize the night-waking and maximize your ability to cope.

Tank baby up during the day

As babies become more active and interested in their world during the day, they may be reluctant to take time out for breastfeeding. They make up for missed feedings by nursing more at night, when there's nothing to distract them. If you make it a point to pick baby up and nurse him often during the day, he may sleep longer stretches at night.

Babies who are away from their mothers during the day, because mother is working outside the home, often fall into a pattern of "reverse cycle" nursing, where they do most of their feeding at night while mother is there and take less milk from bottles during the day when she is not available. Working mothers may just have to put up with this. Baby is making up for all the time with mother he missed during the day. Sharing sleep with baby will make these nighttime feedings easier. In fact, mothers can learn to go back to sleep while baby is nursing.

More touch time

Carrying baby in a sling for several hours during the daytime and evening can help to minimize night-waking. As babies develop the ability to crawl and be more independent, they tend to spend less time in touch with mother during daylight hours. But because they are still babies and still very dependent, they make up for the closeness they missed during the day by waking up often to nurse during the night.

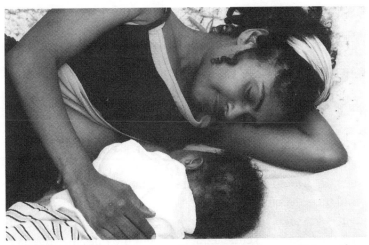

A toddler who wants to nurse all night long may need his mother to set some limits.

Feed baby before you go to bed

If you manage to put your high-need baby down to sleep before you yourself are ready to drop, consider waking baby up for a feeding when you go to bed, especially if it's been a couple of hours since his last feeding. If baby last fed at 9:00 PM and you go to bed at 11:00, he may awaken hungry at midnight. If you wake him and feed him at 11:00, you might get to sleep for three or four hours straight before he wakes you up again.

Toddlers who nurse all night

Even mothers who tolerate their babies waking frequently at night during the first year may be less willing to nurse a one-year-old or an almost-two-year-old all night long. High-need babies and toddlers are known for taking advantage of mom's all-night diner, even if she would prefer to close up shop until breakfast. If all-night nursing is beginning to make you resent your high-need little one, or you are having a hard time functioning on so little sleep, it's time to make some changes.

It is not easy to persuade a persistent night-nurser that he does not need to be attached to the breast to fall asleep or stay asleep, but just as you set limits for your toddler during the day, you can set some limits at nighttime. Your toddler may not like these limits at first, but he can learn to accept them. Be firm, calm, and upbeat. In the second and third year of life, breast-feeding toddlers discover that mothers have needs and feelings, too.

"Night-night, nummies." As your child becomes able to understand simple sentences and concepts, you can introduce an idea such as "Mommy's nummies are sleeping" or "We don't nurse until the sun comes up." Admittedly, a persistent high-need toddler is less likely than the average child to go along with this idea, but issuing a gentle reminder about the rules may dissuade your waking toddler from nursing. Rub his back or offer a drink of water to ease him back into sleep before he has a chance to object.

An alternate comforter. Another strategy to get mom some uninterrupted sleep is to have dad get up with the wakeful toddler and do some creative middle-of-the-night comforting. Usually, older babies and toddlers are nursing at night for comfort, not because they are hungry. They may be ready to learn to accept other forms of soothing when mother needs to sleep. Your toddler may not like this idea, but a patient, persuasive dad can make it work.

Try another sleeping arrangement. Toddlers are less likely to wake to nurse if mother is more than just a few inches away. Try nursing your toddler to sleep on a mattress or futon on the floor next to your bed. Then move yourself into your bed. Some restless sleepers settle better if they are away from other living, breathing bodies.

Watch for signs of stress. When you are trying to set limits on your little one's nighttime nursing, plan on spending more time with your child during the day. If he becomes more clingy during daylight hours or regresses in other ways, he may be telling you that the nighttime changes are more than he can cope with. Don't persist with a bad experiment. Back off and wait a few weeks before trying a new approach.

Benefits of Bedtime Rituals

Parenting a child to sleep, instead of simply putting him to bed, has a mellowing effect on his daytime behavior. The state of relaxation immediately before drifting off to sleep is called the alpha state. It is believed that thoughts which occur during the alpha state are the thoughts most likely to be remembered and carried over into awakening in the morning. If a child goes off to sleep at mother's breast or in father's arms, he feels right. A child who goes to sleep feeling right is more likely to awake feeling right and will begin the next day on a positive note.

Contrast the child who is put down in a crib and left to cry himself to sleep alone. He goes to bed angrily and is therefore likely to awaken in an angry mood. He certainly is destined to "get up on the wrong side of the bed." A little extra energy spent with your child at the end of the day may save you a lot of wasted energy the next day.

Bedtime is also a prime time for planting behavior-mellowing ideas in a child's mind. One creative father of a high-need two-year-old was desperate to calm down his overactive son. He made a tape of soothing environmental sounds: a babbling brook, waves on the beach, flute and harp music in the background, and the soft voice of father narrating a fairy tale that portrayed nice animals in the forest who did nice things for each other all day long. This father's child went to sleep calmly and awoke calmly.

Parents may also use the parenting-to-bed ritual to plant ethical thoughts in a child's mind. This is best accomplished for a toddler by narrating simple fairy tales which contain moral lessons. Older children enjoy just lying in bed and talking with a parent. A lot will be said then that otherwise might be lost.

REFERENCES

Sears, W. 1999. NIGHTTIME PARENTING. Schaumburg, IL. La Leche League International.

Weissbluth, M. and Liel, K. 1983. Sleep patterns, attention span and infant temperament. *J Dev Behav Pediatr* 4:34.

CHAPTER TEN

How to Avoid Burnout

"I can't handle this any longer. I'm not enjoying motherhood. I can't cope, but I have to." These are real feelings shared by caring mothers who are exhausted and approaching the point of burnout.

What is burnout? Every profession demands a certain level of energy from its practitioners. When the demands of a profession exceed an individual's available energy, that person begins to "burn out" and can no longer adequately function within his or her profession. Burnout in the mothering profession means that for a variety of reasons, the demands for your energy exceed your supply. Your ability to cope wears thinner and thinner, and the small amount of energy you have left dwindles to a bare minimum. In short, you are surviving but not thriving. Parenting the high-need child and the lack of sleep that goes with the job are frequent causes of mother burnout.

The main goal of the attachment style of parenting is that you enjoy your child. Burnout keeps you from reaching this goal. Understanding the causes of maternal burnout can help you recognize its warning signs as well as take preventive measures to avoid it.

Causes of Burnout

Perhaps the number one reason why burnout is so common is the Supermom myth. Modern mothers are expected to do so much for so many with little support. In those critical few months after birth, many mothers are not permitted the luxury of being just a mother. In fact, the culture relays the subtle message that "only mothering" is a bit demeaning for the modern woman who has so many other options. Shortly after birth, many mothers are expected to resume their previous roles as loving and giving wives, gourmet cooks, keepers of immaculate houses, gracious hostesses, and contributors to the family income. The baby meanwhile is expected to fit conveniently into this lifestyle. Life in the fast lane and motherhood are often incompatible, even with modern labor-saving devices.

What is even more exhausting to the new mother is that she often enters motherhood with no real role models to follow and without an extended family to turn to for immediate advice and help. Today's mother is alone. All those convenient appliances make poor company, and they have nothing to teach a new mother about babies or about parenting. Many women enter the mothering profession with inadequate preparation, unrealistic expectations, and a lack of coping skills.

Babies are not to blame

Along with the Supermom myth comes the assumption that the baby is always to blame for maternal burnout. In my experience, this is usually not the case. Although it is true that having a high-need baby contributes to exhaustion, I have rarely seen a case of burnout that could be attributed solely to the baby. If you look into each situation carefully, there is usually some other factor that drains away the mother's energy, diverting it from what she should be doing (or wants to be doing) to what her own expectations and those of others require her to be doing.

The mother and baby are designed to operate as a unit. The supply of energy needed for the mother to meet the baby's demands will be available as long as two conditions are met:

- The mother is allowed and encouraged to operate in an environment that allows her intuitive mothering skills to develop.
- Other demands do not drain away her energy.

Burnout is more likely to occur in highly motivated mothers. You have to be on fire before you can get burned out. Burnout is more common in women who strive to be the perfect mother and want to do the things that are best for their babies. I mention this to alleviate the fear that some mothers express: "I must not be a good mother because I have these burned-out feelings." I have a real interest in maternal burnout because I realize that many mothers who are attracted to the attachment style of parenting are mothers who, because they want very much to do what's best for their babies, are at risk for burnout. The attachment style of parenting does not cause burnout, but practicing it in an unsupportive environment can raise the risk.

Mother's stress test

Many factors predispose mothers and fathers to burn out. These include:

- A history of difficulty in coping with stress and a tendency toward depression as a reaction to major changes
- Ambivalent feelings during pregnancy, especially about how the child will interfere with parents' lifestyle
- High recognition in a career before becoming a mother

- Poor prenatal preparation and unrealistic expectations of what babies are like
- Lack of role models for attachment parenting; lack of a good role model in the mother's own mother
- A stressful labor and delivery that did not go according to mother's expectations
- Medical problems at birth which separated mother and baby
- A high-need baby
- Mismatch of temperaments between mother and baby (for example, a fussy baby and a mother with a low tolerance for fussing)
- Marital discord and the expectation that a child will solve the problems
- An uninvolved father
- A highly motivated and compulsive mother
- A mother committed to too many outside activities
- A move or extensive remodeling or redecorating
- Illness in mother, father, or baby
- Financial pressures
- A barrage of conflicting baby care advice
- Successive babies who are close in age, that is, less than two years apart
- Family discord, for example, problems with older children.

Mother burnout is rarely the result of only one of these factors. It usually involves a combination of factors which have a cumulative effect. Burnout is usually a problem that involves the whole family. Rarely is it the mother's problem alone.

Recognizing the Early Warning Signs

There is a saying in medicine that the earlier an illness is recognized, the milder the medicine and the more effective the treatment. In my office, I place a red star at the top of the chart of a baby whose mother exhibits a history with several of the risk factors listed above. This is to remind me that this mother is at risk for burning out and that preventive "medicine" should be administered.

The earliest warning sign of impending burnout is the feeling that you are not enjoying your child. This indicates that you and your child are not in harmony with each other. Harmony between parent and child is absolutely vital in achieving the real benefit of attachment style parenting—enjoying your child.

Another red flag is the feeling, "I'm not a good mother." Occasional feelings of shaky confidence are normal in the mothering profession. These feelings flow naturally from a sincere love for your child. The more you care for another person, the more vulnerable you are to feeling inadequate in that relationship. But when these feelings of inadequacy persist and increase, you should seek help—before your confidence is totally shaken and alternative forms of self-fulfillment have enticed you to withdraw from your child.

Survival Tips That Will Lower Your Risk

If you have several of the above risk factors or have experienced early warning signs of burnout, you can take precautions to prevent your feelings from developing into full-scale burnout. You can lessen your chances of burning out.

Prepare yourself

During your pregnancy, give careful consideration to how your new baby will change your lifestyle, especially if you have an exciting, prestigious career from which you receive lots of recognition. This is especially important if you have ambivalent feelings about your desire or ability to totally immerse yourself in your baby. Whether you plan to return to work after baby is born or temporarily give up your career while your baby is small, your life will change in ways that are hard to anticipate.

Join a support group in order to develop realistic expectations of what babies are like. Many new mothers don't realize how time-consuming a new baby actually is; a tiny baby can turn a predictable, organized lifestyle topsy-turvy. "Nobody told me it would be this way" is a common statement from mothers who had unrealistic expectations of the mothering profession.

A major part of your preparation is getting your husband involved early in your pregnancy, as well as during labor, delivery, and the postpartum period. In my experience the most common cause of mother burnout is an uninvolved father.

Practice the attachment style of parenting

Attachment parenting helps you get in harmony with your baby. It widens your acceptance level, makes your expectations more realistic, and generally increases your confidence. Restraining your responses to your baby leads to chronic disenchantment with the whole mothering role. The attachment style of parenting gives an added boost to maternal stamina with an increase in prolactin, the perseverance hormone.

Know your limits

One night I was giving a talk on "immersion mothering" which involves really getting tuned into your child. After the talk, a grandmother came up to me and said, "Dr. Sears, do you realize that 'immersion' means getting in over your head?" Mothers who are burning out may feel as if they are in over their heads.

Mothers should not only have realistic expectations of their babies; they also need to have realistic expectations of their own tolerance level. Mothers vary greatly in their ability to cope with a high-need baby. This statement is not meant to be critical of mothers. It is simply a fact. Some mothers tolerate stress better than others. Some are frazzled by one crying baby while others are not ruffled even by several babies and children crawling all over them like a human jungle gym. It is important to be honest with yourself and accept your coping abilities for what they are. Do not let yourself get into situations that require you to go beyond your personal tolerance level. For example, if your first baby is a high-need baby and you do not have a high level of tolerance for fussing, it would probably be unwise to add to the strain by having another baby right away. Be wise enough to admit that in your particular situation, spacing your children farther apart will lessen your risk of burning out.

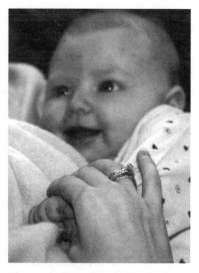

The main benefit of attachment style parenting is enjoying your baby more.

During my years as a pediatrician and father I have been amazed at how many mothers cope so well (at least on the surface) with the many stresses of child-rearing and family life. But I have also observed that many women do not know and accept their own limits. This is especially true of highly motivated mothers whose desire to give of themselves often completely overpowers their ability to know that they are giving out. This may be a result, in part, of the hormonal effects of attachment parenting. Mothers vary in their ability to hear and heed their own distress signals. They also may not know how to react to these signals once they recognize them.

How Fathers Can Help Mothers Avoid Burnout

Just as mothers are not noted for their ability to recognize the signs of impending burnout, fathers also are not known for their sensitivity to their wives' distress signals. The most common cause of maternal burnout is an uninvolved father.

Fathers, be sensitive to those factors that put your wife at risk for burning out, and be alert for the early warning signs mentioned above. Don't wait for your wife to tell you that she can't cope. Wives seldom confide their ambivalent feelings to their husbands; they don't want to appear weak or to risk shattering their husband's image of them as a perfect mother.

Harmony is as important in the mother-father relationship as it is in the mother-child relationship. To be sensitive to imminent burnout you have to be tuned in to the stresses in your individual family situation which compete with your wife's mothering energy. For example, as an involved father you can create an atmosphere which makes it easier for your wife to breastfeed successfully. By "mothering the mother" you can help her develop a positive breastfeeding relationship.

Father's involvement is especially important if you have been blessed with a high-need child. A father who is not involved early on may never become comfortable with consoling the fussy baby, handling a temper tantrum, or disciplining an unruly child. Lack of early involvement has a snowballing effect. The less involved you are, the less comfortable you are with your effectiveness as a father. This can lead some men to withdraw from both the high-need child and the family situation and retreat into interests outside the home where they feel more comfortable and competent. The combination of a high-need child, a burned-out mother, and a withdrawn father can lead to the collapse of the entire family structure.

The mother of a high-need child who was nearing the point of burnout recently shared an example of this kind of situation with me. She confided, "By the time my husband comes home I am a wreck. However, he expects our child to be bathed, in her pajamas, and ready for bed. The quicker we can get her off to bed so that we can settle down for a quiet evening with just the two of us, the more pleased he is." This is a classic situation: Mother is worn out by the end of the day, and the high-need child needs some prime time with dad in the evening. Dad comes home from work to his castle and discovers that neither

"I'm Not
Going to Let that Baby Run My Life"
"When I was pregnant I set down some rules that
I planned to follow after our child was born. I wasn't
going to let a baby manipulate me or run our lives.
I wanted to get her on a schedule as soon as possible.
I was determined not to be one of those mothers
whose baby was hanging on her all the time.

"My labor was long and painful. The baby kept spitting up formula during the month after her birth, so
I tried breastfeeding. I had been given a shot to dry
up my milk so I needed to use a nursing supple-
menter to bring my milk back in. By eight months,
I had a good milk supply, and the baby was demanding to be held and nursed all the time. I didn't want
her to get into the habit of needing to be held all the
time. So I weaned her cold turkey at nine months.
I can't get anything done. I feel trapped but I can't
resign. I have tried to let her cry it out but I can't
stand to listen to her. I had no parenting models to
follow. My mother spanked me whenever I got out of
line. Kristine has become an intensely angry baby."

Dr. Sears comments: *This mother is burned out.*
She was at high risk from early on: poor parenting models,
unrealistic expectations, a traumatic birth experience,
mother-baby separation after birth, and an injection that
suppresses the natural maternal hormones. This mother
and baby never got in harmony with each other. The baby
demanded the attachment style of parenting until she got
it, but the mother was reluctant. The mother would have

profited from a counselor who could have pointed out the mismatch between her expectations and her baby's temperament.

Some mothers feel that they are losing control of the situation when they are open to their babies. Over the course of several months in which I advised this mother to use the attachment style of parenting, I reassured her that responding to her baby would eventually pay off, but because she was playing "catch-up," it might take some time. She and her baby finally began to enjoy each other, and her closing comments were, "I wish somebody had pointed this out to me a lot earlier."

the queen nor the little princess is up to regal behavior. A father who has not been consistently involved with the child does not know how to handle the situation.

Early evening is a particularly stressful time for many families. It is a time when mother's energy is giving out and father wants to wind down. The child, however, is winding up in anticipation of the change from daytime with mother to an evening with father. This situation is further compounded by the fact that children are often the most tired and therefore the least enjoyable at that time of the day or evening.

The attachment style of parenting works only if childcare is shared by both parents. A father who is sensitive to the risk of mother burnout will frequently administer preventive medicine: "I'll take over. You do something just for yourself."

An uninvolved father once sent his wife into my office for some counseling with the subtle message that "it must be her fault that we have a demanding child whom she can't handle." Since father sent mother in for some treatment, I felt that it was my professional duty to prescribe the most effective medicine I knew of. I gave mother a prescription and said, "Now be sure your husband fills this for you." The prescription read,

"Administer one dose of caring husband and involved father three times a day and before bedtime until symptoms subside."

The carry-over effect of burnout

Maternal burnout often carries over into the marriage. A burned-out mother becomes a burned-out wife. Her feelings of exhaustion and ineffectiveness often mushroom into general feelings of inadequacy as a person. Depression sets in. She pays less attention to her own grooming and appearance. She may vent her frustrations on her husband, especially if she senses a lack of involvement and support from him. Many men tend to withdraw rather than increase their involvement. Because both partners are insensitive to each other's needs, they drift apart and the result is marriage burnout as well as maternal burnout. Quite honestly, dads, this is why involved fathering is such a good investment for you. By keeping your wife from burning out, your marriage will mature, and you yourself will ultimately profit.

Be sensitive to each other

Just as fathers are often not sensitive to the early signs of maternal burnout, mothers may not confide in their husbands. They may be unwilling to release their child into their husband's care, or they may not be assertive about their husbands playing an active role in childcare. Without harmony and mutual sensitivity it is very difficult for families to survive the pressures of parenting a high-need child. Fathers, be sensitive and anticipate the new mother's needs. Mothers, be open to your husband's suggestion that your reserves are exhausted and something has to give. Mothers can sit down and make an "I need help" list. Write down all the daily chores which compete with mothering for your energy: housework, cooking, errands, etc. Tell your husband exactly where you need help in all these areas and be open to his ideas, especially if he suggests that several of these seemingly important daily tasks don't have to get done.

Define Your Priorities

Very early in your mothering career you will realize that you cannot be all things to all people and that a list of priorities is necessary for survival. Be realistic about how much time and energy you must spend on your family situation, especially if you have a high-need child or a large family with close-in-age children. Sit down and make a list of all those daily activities that drain away your energies. With the support of your husband, scratch as many of these activities off the list as possible. For example, an exhausted mother recently told me that she was a compulsive housekeeper until one day she looked at the kitchen floor and realized, "That floor doesn't have feelings. No one's life is going to be affected if that floor doesn't get scrubbed every day. My baby is a baby for a very short time, and she has feelings." This is part of maturing as a mother. You have to realize that if ten things need to be done and you only have energy for eight of them, you should only do eight things. Just be sure to include all the ones with feelings.

Do something for yourself

It is unrealistic for mothers to think that one role can satisfy all their needs for fulfillment. This is a high-risk situation for burnout. An unhappy mother is no good to anyone, especially herself. Realistically, babies are takers and mothers are givers, and babies will continue to take until their own needs are completely filled. Babies are designed this way so that they can grow up to be loving, giving adults. But a mother cannot give continuously without being recharged periodically. Most mothers, especially those with high-need children, need to discipline themselves to take some time to do things they want to do—not just things they have to do. Dedicated mothers of high-need children are not always able to admit that they need time off, especially if they are isolated in a situation in which taking time off seems impossible. Oftentimes it is necessary for a sensitive and caring husband, a friend, or a health care professional to step in and release the mother for a bit of time off. As one mother told me, "I just needed someone to give me permission to take some time for me. I felt that my child needed me constantly." Intervention like this is aimed at helping mother and father nurture themselves in order that they can better nurture their children. This is not meant to encourage a mother to become selfish or uncaring about her child but rather to help her develop staying power so that she can continue to mother in the way the child was designed to be mothered.

One of my patients who had been a concert pianist prior to having her first baby provides a good example of a mother taking time for herself. She was blessed with a high-need baby and had made a commitment to mothering, so she devoted her full time and energy to her baby. She also received help from a highly involved father and supportive friends. Her baby was the type of high-need baby who demanded mother's full energy twenty-four hours a day. Nevertheless, this mother had the wisdom to take a half-hour each day to sit down at her piano and enjoy her skill. Her child would fuss while she played, but she had decided that this was her time and she deserved it. She did not leave her child alone; he was allowed to play with his toys in the same room. After a while the child began to respect mother's private time, and he sensed that she felt better afterwards and that he benefited in the long run.

In another family situation, the mother refused to take any time off, but the father had the wisdom and insight to recognize early signs of burnout. Twice a week he came home early from work and insisted that his wife go down to the health spa and relax. Two things helped this mother to accept the idea: She trusted her husband's wisdom and judgment (an example of family harmony), and she felt comfortable leaving the baby in the husband's arms since he had been involved in the baby's care from early on. Even in societies where babies are almost constantly in arms, they are often in the arms of family members other than the mother.

Another mother put it this way: "I feel that even after birth my labor never really stopped and that I'm still pregnant with a two-year-old. My life is a circle that revolves around her. What I need is a square which encloses her circle but leaves some corners just for me."

Nighttime Parenting and Family Burnout

Children's sleep difficulties can place great stress on a family and contribute to child abuse and broken marriages. Your child's sleep problem becomes a family problem when his frequent night-waking exceeds your ability to cope. What happens when you have reviewed all possible causes of night-waking and tried all the tips for inducing sleep and nothing works? Occasionally I talk to a mother who is trying to be a perfect nighttime parent but as a result is so exhausted that her effectiveness during the day as a mother, wife, and person is greatly diminished. There simply is not enough energy to go around if the mother is up with the child all night and is expected to meet everyone's needs during the day. I find this a most difficult situation in which to counsel parents, and I usually start by saying, "You have a problem and you're not going to like any of the solutions for it, but we must admit that you have to do something. Something has to go. The whole family is losing." If being the perfect nighttime parent wipes out your effectiveness during the day, you should recognize this as a red flag which indicates that you need to make some changes, the sooner the better. (See "The All-Night Nurser" in Chapter 9 for suggestions.)

Difficult decisions are often necessary in the growth of a new family. A realistic assessment and acceptance of your tolerance level is absolutely necessary for achieving the main benefit of the attachment style of parenting—enjoying your child.

CHAPTER ELEVEN

Disciplining the High-Need Child

"She's so stubborn, she just won't mind," complained the mother of a high-need two-year-old. Because every child is unique and every parent is unique as well, there are as many styles of discipline as there are high-need children. In this chapter, I will present a style of discipline that has worked well in our family and in other families in my practice.

Because high-need children are notoriously resistant to punishment as a discipline technique, the goal of this chapter is to help parents create the atmosphere and attitudes that make punishment less necessary. When you understand that discipline depends on the trust you establish with your child, you can use your parental authority wisely, and you will have many more options for disciplining your child.

Why High-Need Children Are More Difficult to Discipline

The temperament traits that may be an asset to the older high-need child are the same ones that get the young child into trouble. Because these children are so intense, they go at things in a big way and attempt tasks that are beyond their developmental capabilities. Many a worn-out mother has spent the day chasing a high-need child who seems to be trying to rearrange the entire house. These children tend to be impulsive; they rush headlong into action without stopping first to form a game plan. This impulsiveness leads them into trouble. These children, because they are so acutely aware of their environment, are intensely curious. They want to catch anything that moves, turn anything that revolves, and push anything that will go. They are quick to protest restrictions imposed on their exploring. High-need children are not known for their caution. They tend to be climbers and hangers and are the children most likely to dart out into the street because something interesting is on the other side.

"She's so defiant," complained a worn-out mother who had shouted "no" a thousand times with little effect on her child's behavior. Many high-need children have a strong ego which creates clashes with their caregivers. "I do it myself" is their battle cry. Inner pride, confidence, and assertiveness are characteristic especially of high-need children who are products of the attachment style of parenting. These qualities indicate a high level of self-esteem. Other methods of child rearing that encourage parents not to give in to their child's needs and demands squelch the high-need child's personality development and cause her not to trust her environment or herself. This can lead to fragile self-esteem.

Toddler impulsiveness

Here's how the mind of a toddler processes your "no." A curious and impulsive toddler does not yet have the wisdom to discern which knobs are harmful and which are not. She wants to

Get down on the child's level to communicate effectively.

touch them all. When her first few attempts to reach the knob get a "no" from mother (a maternal reaction that takes approximately one millisecond), she soon learns that "no" means she should stop whatever she is doing. Mom may also explain, "Don't touch, that will hurt Susie!" Children with easier temperaments get the point rather quickly; after a few interactions like this, all the parent has to do is look at the child sternly, and this docile toddler complies.

High-need children need stronger "law enforcement" accompanying the no. Words alone won't do the job. This child needs to be picked up immediately, looked squarely in the eye, and gently but authoritatively removed from the dangerous situation. The parent may have to intervene and prevent the child from touching the knob many times before the child can restrain her own impulses. "No" is most effective if followed up with redirection—something positive for the child to do instead.

Trying parents' patience

It is easy to become frustrated when you feel that you're just not getting through to your child. But don't give up. Your child does want to please you, but it takes longer to shape the behavior of high-need children. This is why the early months of taking charge of the fussy baby are so important. The trusting relationship established when mother and father respond to baby's needs is the foundation for later discipline. It will help you avoid turning toddler discipline into a confrontation of wills. The attachment style of parenting allows you to be firm but patient with your child because you are operating from a basis of trust.

Parents who have developed a strong sensitivity toward their child will discover that the child is also sensitive to their moods. Discipline problems are most likely to occur during times of parental stress, when parents' reserves of patience are at their lowest. Parents have often told me, "When I'm feeling good, my child is good."

Tantrums

Most high-need children are prone to temper tantrums between one and two years of age. They protest violently at any limits imposed on their impulsive behavior. Temper tantrums are the result of two feelings: the child's own frustration with having to conform to the will of another and her anger at being out of control.

High-need children lack the inner controls necessary to handle such strong emotions. They do not have the verbal skills to express their feelings in words so they do so in actions. The most terrifying of all tantrums, both to parent and to child, are breath-holding spells in which the child cries so hard and becomes so angry that toward the end of the cry she appears to hold her breath, turns blue, becomes limp, and seems to be on the verge of fainting. Fortunately, just when parents are on the verge of frantic helplessness, the child resumes breathing. She does no harm to herself but leaves her parents a wreck. Mothers of high-need children will often describe the tantrum behavior

Discipline depends on the trust you establish with your child.

as "becoming unglued." Keeping your child from falling apart and gluing her back together again are challenging tasks for parents of high-need children. Nobody enjoys a temper tantrum, so working at preventing them is important.

"But how do I handle these tantrums?" is the plea of helpless parents. I don't believe in ignoring tantrums because children need someone in authority to help them regain control. Hold the struggling child firmly and lovingly with your arms around her, restraining her flailing arms. Accompany this with a reassuring voice saying, "You are out of control, and I am just going to hold you tight until you feel better." Even the most defiant child will usually turn down her runaway engine and submit to someone more in control. She will melt into your arms as if thanking you for rescuing her from herself. If holding her tightly only makes your child fight more, try standing by and reassuring her with words: "You're mad because you can't go outside today. That's no fun. I understand." These strategies for dealing with tantrums give a child the tools she needs to learn to control herself eventually. Issuing ultimatums ("Now get

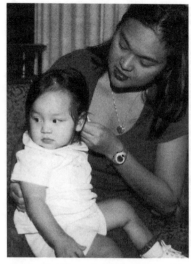

Breastfeeding should continue until your baby outgrows the need.

up off that floor before I count to three!") asks her to get herself under control without teaching her how to do this.

"I want" or "I won't"?

If brought up in an environment that complements their temperamental traits, high-need children's strong personalities become an asset. But the "I want" in their personalities is often perceived by parents as "I won't." For example, a two-year-old happily playing at her friend's house feels so right and fits so well within the current situation that she protests loudly when mother comes in and announces that it is time to go. This child deeply wants to continue doing what she's doing and does not easily yield her will to that of another. If mother perceives her daughter's protests as defiance and responds by asserting her authority, a clash of wills ensues, and the issue is no longer that it's time to go home. Instead, both mother and daughter are focused on who will win the battle. In this situation, both sides are destined to lose. The child perceives her mother's authority as capricious and unfeeling. Mother must now deal with a child who is truly defiant, not just a child who doesn't want to go home yet. The hardest thing about disciplining a high-need child is instilling a healthy respect for authority without either squelching the strength of her will or turning her into an angry child.

How should parents handle this kind of situation? Recognize that a high-need child needs help with making transitions and help her release herself from her present activity. Fifteen minutes before it's time to go, you let her know that she will have to stop playing soon. Ten minutes before you want to leave, you sit down with her and help her pick up the toys she's been playing with and get ready to say goodbye. You remind her of what she can do when you get home and help her look forward to the next activity. All of this takes more time than just saying "Let's go," but it is a lot less stressful than pulling rank to make your child "mind."

There are times when you want your child to obey you quickly and without question, for example, in situations when the health or safety of your child or another child is on the line. Save the big guns for occasions like these. Your child will know by your emotion and tone of voice that this time she must do as you say.

An Approach to Disciplining the High-Need Child

"I can't get her to mind. The harder I spank, the worse she gets," complained a frustrated mother. Parents often confuse discipline with punishment.

Punishment is an external force, applied because the child has strayed from the straight and narrow path. Punishment is really only one form of discipline and not a very effective one in most situations. I wish parents would think beyond punishment. Disciplining a child means shaping something within the child that motivates her to stay on the right path. She feels right when she acts right and does not feel right when she acts wrongly.

Creating the attitude and the atmosphere

One way to do this is to create an atmosphere in the home that makes punishment less necessary. Toward the end of a child's first year, the parents' role as nurturer expands into that of authority figure and designer of a safe environment. To avoid having to say "no" all the time, you remove the breakables, put safety plugs in the electrical outlets, and place gates in front of the stairs. You are using your authority wisely—you are making dangerous options unavailable to your child. You are also saving that important word "no" for truly dangerous situations. At the same time, you also provide fun things for her to do—a special cupboard in the kitchen that she is allowed to empty, lightweight foam balls that are okay to chase through the house. Just as you responded to your infant's need for assistance in calming herself, you respond to your toddler's need to explore by making her environment stimulating but safe.

All of these actions reinforce your child's trust in your adult authority. When you must actively step in and stop or redirect what she is doing, she will be willing to follow your lead. Trust is the best basis for parental authority. When the impulsive toddler goes after the knob on the gas stove and you descend upon her with a firm "no," you are demanding that your child yield her will to yours. You want her to do this not because you are bigger and more powerful than she is, but because she trusts you unconditionally. The stronger the child's will, the greater the amount of trust required.

What's wrong with spanking?

In my experience, high-need children resist the effects of corporal punishment. Spanking is supposed to operate on the behavior modification principle of reinforcement. An undesirable action receives an undesirable reaction—spanking. High-need children often do not make the connection between spanking and the self-control they need to exercise to avoid spanking. They are not being willfully stubborn; they just don't get the connection between their behavior and being hurt and humiliated by a spanking. You, as the parent and authority figure, must anticipate situations in which your child will have trouble exercising self-control and then either avoid them or help your child cope. Children may not only fail to connect a spanking with the bad behavior, they may also connect the negative feelings that accompany a spanking with the parent who administered it. This will make it more difficult for a parent to guide the child in the future.

Realistic expectations

Disciplining the high-need child requires that you have realistic expectations of what your child can cope with. You should not impose demands on a child that are beyond her, either developmentally or temperamentally. Expecting an impulsive toddler to walk down the aisle of a supermarket without grabbing all those tempting delights off the shelf is totally unrealistic. Parents of high-need children usually are

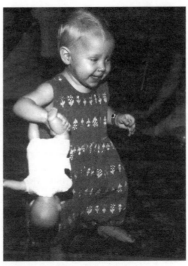

High-need babies often grow into active toddlers.

more accepting of a wider spectrum of childish behavior. They chalk up the small problems to their child's personality and avoid high risk situations such as supermarkets which usually bring out the worst in parent and child.

If taking your child to the supermarket is unavoidable, be prepared to be creative in your discipline by playing games such as "Mommy's Helper." Show your child what you want to get off the shelf and let her grab it and put it into the basket for you. Give her lots of recognition for her help and patiently help her put away any extra items that land in your shopping cart. This does take more time, but it's worth it, both in the short run and as an investment in your child's future.

A loving approach

When you are working on shaping the behavior of the high-need child, use lots of eye contact. This body language tells the child that you are truly talking from your heart and that you want her to make good choices because you love her. When you persist with this approach to disciplining high-need children, they develop respect for your fairness and wisdom.

This approach to discipline is not lenient or permissive. It requires the investment of time, but it gives your child the tools needed to work with others and maintain good relationships. Loving discipline is not about bending your high-need child's will to agree with yours. It looks to the future and prepares your child for life.

REFERENCES

Sears, W. and Sears, M. 1995. *The Discipline Book.* Boston: Little, Brown and Co.

CHAPTER TWELVE

The Pay-Off

"It's been a long tough struggle, but we're finally beginning to cash in on our investment," explained the parents of a high-need two-year-old. Parenting the high-need child has a high investment/return ratio. A lot is asked of the parents of a high-need child, but the rewards are great.

When parents are open to their baby's temperament, accept his needs, and develop a parenting style that works for the whole family, they bring out the best in the child. This challenge, along with the response from the child, also brings out the best in the parents. The parents mature and grow along with their child. As a father of a high-need child once told me, "Nothing matures a parent more than the challenge of getting in harmony with a high-need child." By "mature" this father meant more than adding gray hairs.

The Outcome

Parents will often ask, "How will my child turn out? Is he going to be a hyperactive child? Will he ever leave our bed? Will he ever wean?" High-need children vary greatly, but an analysis of the cases of high-need babies that I have run into shows some general trends.

High-need babies can indeed become a joy to their parents. Responsive parenting channels their behavior into positive personality traits. The responsive parenting styles discussed in this book that I have found contribute to a good outcome for high-need infants are:

- Unrestricted breastfeeding
- Openness and responsiveness to baby's cries, cues, and temperament
- Sharing sleep with parents
- Babywearing
- An involved and supportive father
- Parents involved in support systems that affirm their parenting choices.

The high-need children whose parents followed these guidelines became sensitive, caring, trusting, fearless individuals.

Problem baby, problem child?

To help answer the question of whether difficult babies turn out to be problem children, researchers designed the New York Longitudinal Study, which began in 1956 (Thomas et al. 1968). They followed 136 children from early infancy into later childhood. They attempted to categorize the infants as either easy or difficult based upon nine categories of temperament: activity level, rhythmicity of biologic functions, ease of adaptability, approach-withdrawal reactions to new situations, sensory threshold, mood (primarily positive or negative mood), intensity of mood, distractibility, and persistence or attention span. The easy child in their study was characterized by biologic regularity, an easy approach to new situations, a generally positive mood, and adaptability. The difficult children in the study showed biologic irregularity, usually withdrew from new situations, had many negative moods and expressed them with marked intensity, and were slow to adapt to change.

The results of this study showed that infants labeled as difficult babies exhibited a higher incidence of behavior

Developing a parenting style that works for the whole family brings rewards.

disorders as older children, mainly in the areas of sleep, mood, discipline, and peer relationships. While the study did show a correlation between infant behavior and later difficulties, it was not a perfect correlation. Easy babies did sometimes turn out to be difficult children and vice versa. The authors concluded only that difficult babies are at a higher risk of becoming more difficult children.

While the researchers did not intend to study the effects of different parenting styles, the study did show that no one parenting style worked with every child all the time. The most successful parent-child relationship was one in which the mother showed both consistency and flexibility and used a combination of attitudes and practices in her parenting. In other words, the babies with the best outcome were the ones whose mothers were flexible in responding to their needs. The study showed that the child with the good outcome often had parents who never considered him to have a behavioral disturbance; they felt instead that the child's troublesome behavior was the expression of his own personality, which needed modifying. The child who had a poor outcome had parents who interacted with him in a way that was excessively stressful, inconsistent, and confusing to the child.

Benefits of attachment parenting for high-need children

Enhanced development. High-need babies who are in harmony with their environment often reach developmental milestones sooner. There is an energy-sparing effect on the baby because the parents provide harmony in the baby's environment. This prevents the baby from wasting energy overcoming his own internal stress and allows him to use that energy to develop his skills. Researchers who have studied infant care patterns in other cultures have made some interesting observations about infants reared in almost continuous contact with their mothers (Geber 1958). These mothers carry their babies with them in slings. The babies are given free access to the breast and seem to nurse continuously. The babies are constantly in somebody's arms. When mother's arms wear out, the extended family is around to play "pass the baby." The babies seldom cry because their needs are anticipated and promptly responded to. Babies and mothers sleep together and nurse through the night. The researchers noticed that infants who received this attachment style of parenting were clearly precocious in both neuromuscular and cognitive development when compared with infants of more "advanced" cultures.

I can tell a lot about the strength of the parent-child attachment by observing the toddler at play. Picture two toddlers in a playroom with their mothers. The high-need toddler who is not strongly attached to his parent will often flit from toy to toy, spending very little time with any one toy. He has a poor attention span and seldom acknowledges his mother. The high-need child of attachment parents also flits from toy to toy, but he studies them more attentively and periodically checks into home base (mother) for reassurance that all is well. Both toddlers are showing independence, but the first toddler's independence lacks direction. The second toddler learns more from his explorations. He is more secure and free to explore the unknown because of his close attachment to his responsive parents.

Giving children. High-need babies who are matched with giving parents become giving children. Good takers later become good givers because giving is the style they are accustomed to. These children share more easily—something which comes hard to many children. They also seem more concerned about the needs and rights of the other children around them. Their parents have achieved a healthy balance in their giving, neither overindulging nor restraining. This is in contrast to so-called "spoiled" children who are often the products of inappropriate giving, either too much (which can keep a child from becoming independent) or too little.

Sensitivity. Because high-need babies have grown up in an environment where their caregivers were sensitive to their needs, they become children who are more sensitive to the needs of other children. A crying baby or another child getting hurt bothers these children. Why? Because that is the response they learned when they were crying and hurting. Parents are the prime recipients of this sensitivity. One mother shared with me the story of a particularly down day when she was crying. Her three-year-old daughter (a former high-need baby) hurried over, put her arms around her mother, and said from her heart, "Don't cry, Mommy. I'll help you."

Feeling right. When harmony is achieved between a high-need baby and giving parents, a feeling of inner rightness overtakes the child and becomes part of his nature. These children exude a feeling of peace, as if they are right for their world and the world is right for them. A peaceful child is better able to handle the many stresses that will come his way during his normal growth and development. He will continually strive to regain this feeling of rightness by modifying his environment and his reactions accordingly. The child who has grown up continually not feeling right is at a higher risk for becoming a generally angry child, the type who seems always to have a chip on his shoulder.

Direction. Demanding babies often become impulsive children, and it is this unbridled impulsiveness that gets them in trouble. Parents will often ask if their fussy baby is likely to become a hyperactive child. Most parents of hyperactive children do report that they "came wired this way." Yes, fussy babies do have a higher chance of becoming hyperactive children. This is where the parents' perseverance in gentling their high-need baby really pays off. Children whose parents help them learn self-control in early infancy seem to have more control of themselves later on.

Parents who have practiced the attachment style of parenting know their hyperactive child so well that they are better able to channel the child's impulsive and destructive behavior. Without this foundation, parents flounder in a sea of uncertainty, and their child is turned over to the advice of specialists and experts rather than being guided by intuitive parents. Hyperactive children who do not have the foundation of attachment parenting are often very angry, though this may not be evident on the surface. I feel that anger is one of the most overlooked feelings behind most behavior problems. In my experience the most difficult hyperactive child to deal with is one who operates from a basis of anger. One of my goals in writing this book is to help children avoid feeling angry. Fussy babies who are destined to be hyperactive children, but who have received attachment parenting, operate from a basis of trust rather than anger.

"What About the Other Kids?"

"Katie, who is four years old, has weathered the storm caused by her high-need baby sister with some interesting effects. She did not know any other baby before Megan, our high-need baby, so she came to assume that every baby was like Megan. This became evident when she played with her dolls. The dolls always cried a lot, and she always comforted them as I did Megan. She would hold them and rock or nurse them and repeat my exact words, 'Come on, honey. Don't cry, Mommy's here.' Katie was often involved in soothing and quieting her dolls. This was a wonderful sight for me to witness.

"Then a close friend had a baby who was the epitome of perfect. He hardly ever cries, never gets upset, and never screams. Katie asked why our baby couldn't be more like the other baby. I felt bad, but I could certainly understand her question.

"At least this experience has given her a realistic expectation of what babies can be like some of the time. It has also shown her that we don't abandon each other in times of need, no matter how frustrated we are. In her play I see that she has mastered some mothering techniques that I had to learn by trial and error. I hope that mothering will be easier for her because of this, especially if she has a high-need infant."

> **Dr. Sears comments:** *Parents may wonder how a fussy baby affects the older children in the family. Do they grow up thinking that all babies are fussy? This story is a good example of how an older child picks up on mother's modeling. It was important that Katie learn that not all babies are fussy like her little sister; otherwise there could be a damaging effect on her attitude toward motherhood. From watching her own mother, Katie has learned to be a giving person.*

Fearlessness. Parents often describe high-need children as fearless because they have grown up in an environment where they had little to fear. "She has no need to fear," said one mother who devoted a great deal of energy to creating a peaceful environment around her high-need baby. The normal fears of early childhood may not be as intense in these children, since they have had help from their parents in learning to deal with anxiety. They carry this fearlessness and peace into later childhood.

Trust. If you were to ask me to use one word to describe the high-need baby who has grown up in a harmonious environment, I would choose the word "trusting." When an infant is trusted, he learns to trust. When a high-need baby grows up in a responsive environment he learns to believe that his needs should and will be properly identified and consistently met. This represents two kinds of trust: The infant trusts that his cues are worthy of being listened to, and he trusts that his caregivers will respond to these cues. He learns to trust himself and the loving people around him. This contributes to his self-esteem and his ability to form trusting relationships with other. Both parents and child profit by simply listening to each other.

Self-esteem. All of the above traits of high-need children contribute to a high level of self-esteem. These harmoniously parented babies feel right about themselves and feel as though they fit into their environment. They eventually turn out to be creative children who give back to their environment the loving, responsive care that their environment gave to them. They make our world a more interesting and peaceful place to live.

The Shutdown Syndrome

Babies who grow up in a less satisfying environment are often slower in their emotional and motor development. This phenomenon is known in pediatric circles as the "deprivation syndrome." High-need babies who do not get the attention they need may show varying degrees of developmental delay as a reaction. I have counseled mothers in this situation. It seems to me that the babies just shut down. I wonder how many high-need babies receiving a level of care that is not adequate for them show subtle effects of shutdown which go undetected.

Part of the shutdown syndrome may be the result of reactive depression. The baby is grieving over the loss of an important relationship, just as adults show physical and emotional changes in reaction to a loss. This reactive depression is carried one step further when the baby's signals are not listened to. Crying is the strongest attachment-promoting behavior a baby has. Can you imagine the depth of grief that overtakes a little person whose cries are not listened to and who possesses limited abilities to compensate for this loss?

The following letter describes the shutdown syndrome and what one mother did to set her baby back on the path to healthy emotional and physical development:

"I was an experienced mother of two, and then along came baby Andy. As a newborn he loved to fall asleep on my chest, listening to my breathing and heartbeat. I was very tired most of the time with a newborn and two other children under four years of age. Consequently Andy rarely made it into the bassinet beside my bed. He just slept with me. He was fun to hold, so I held him throughout the day.

"But Andy grew very quickly. He became too heavy to carry in the carrier so I started putting him in the stroller. He'd be happy for five minutes, but then he'd start crying and wouldn't stop until I picked him up. He was also a restless sleeper, so I started putting him in the crib after nursing him down to sleep.

"When he started crawling I could no longer keep him beside me wherever I went in the house. So I set up the playpen. Every time I put him in it, he got hysterical. I wasn't used to hearing him cry, so by the time I finished waxing the floor or took a shower or whatever, I was a basket case.

"When I put him in the highchair, he ate, played, and really enjoyed it, as long as I fed him and tended to his every need. If I left to fix dinner for us or even to get some more food for him, he would cry and stop eating.

"I called my pediatrician and told him about the crying episodes in the playpen and voiced the fear that my son was becoming a 'mama's boy.' The doctor advised me to leave Andy in the playpen and do my work around the house. He said Andy would eventually give up and quit crying. This was on a Monday. If Andy was still crying by Friday, I was to call back so we could figure out something else, since we couldn't leave him cry for more than five or six days!

"The first day I left him in the playpen he never stopped crying. On the second day, Andy actually made himself vomit. The next morning, as soon as I carried him into the front room and he saw the playpen, he started crying and vomited up all the breast milk from his last nursing. I decided, 'Forget this. I can't do this to him anymore.'

"From this point on, he seemed even more clingy. All he wanted was to be held. He wouldn't nurse very often or for very long. He had dropped from the seventieth percentile to the fortieth on the weight chart at his nine-month checkup. A month later he was down to the twentieth. The pediatrician sent us to the hospital for tests, all of which came out normal.

"A friend suggested I listen to Dr. Sears' radio program. I tuned in to hear a mother asking a question about her high-need baby, and he explained that 'Smart babies don't let their mothers put them down.' As Dr. Sears explained more about high-need babies, I knew I had one. I was so excited! Here was someone who knew about my baby. Maybe it wasn't my fault that he was like that.

"I thought back to the early months when I had always had Andy with me. Then I realized that I had unknowingly pushed him away from me. The crowning blow was letting him cry it out, all by himself. I realized that it was after I had let Andy cry for so long in the playpen that he had stopped eating and started losing weight.

"I started thinking of him as a high-need baby. I bought a back-pack baby carrier. I carried him everywhere. Whether I was doing dishes or talking on the phone, Andy was on my back. I never put him in the high chair. He ate adult food from my plate while sitting on my lap. I nursed him to sleep in my bed. At night I got him out of his crib and into our bed for his 11:00 PM feeding. This was followed by a long cuddle time with us, with lots of touching and little sounds which he would make back to us. He loved it.

"The more little intimacies I initiated with him, the more he began to eat. The happier he was, the less clingy he became. At his next weight check, he had gained four pounds and was now back on the chart. He is good-natured again, laughs a lot, and enjoys life."

Benefits for parents

There are times, I'm sure, when parents feel that there is absolutely no advantage in having a high-need baby. They seem somewhat surprised when I use positive terms such as "blessed with" and "fortunate," but I mean them sincerely. High-need babies, properly parented, can bring out the best in their parents. Parents of high-need babies receive a good return on their investment of time and energy.

Knowing the child better. By being tuned in to their infant's cues, showing unrestrained responses, and evaluating the feedback the infant gives them, parents come to know their child better. They learn what works and what doesn't work. Even mothers who begin their parenting career with shaky intuition gradually become more confident when they go along with the conditions (the attachment style of parenting) that allow their intuition to mature. This confidence is boosted regularly by responses from the infant, and the whole system of parent-child supply and demand operates at a higher, more harmonious level. In short, parents become more sensitive. Mother and father often become more sensitive to each other as well, and their marriage prospers. A stable and fulfilling marriage gives the process of parenting the high-need baby a real head start.

Greater acceptance. Attached parents develop more acceptance of their child's behavior. In addition to building up your sensitivity, you build up your tolerance for this demanding, draining child. This starts with developing realistic expectations of your child's behavior instead of comparing him with other babies. Your child does not behave like the child next door because he is not the child next door. This acceptance of your child's behavior gradually matures into being able to focus more on the positive aspects of his temperament. This comes from having worked so hard to modify the negatives and accentuate the positives. I find that parents of high-need children gradually come to use fewer negative terms in describing their child. The baby graduates from being unpredictable, uncontentable, and unsatisfied to being challenging, interesting, curious, aware, confident, and bright. Some labels such as exhausting and draining seem to stick with high-need children, because they are above-average children and it requires more than the average amount of parental energy to keep up with them. I have noticed that mothers who have both survived and thrived with their high-need babies seem to get a "second wind" every six months or so. This extra boost of energy sees them through those especially trying times when a child is in transition from one developmental stage to the next.

Easier discipline. When parents know their child well, they tend to provide discipline by following the intuitive leading of their hearts rather than choosing a method out of a book and trying their hardest to make the child conform. Parents of high-need children seem to read their children better. They anticipate those situations which get the child in trouble and intuitively and creatively channel the child's impulses into alternative behavior. Because the child feels right, he is more likely to act right. Discipline is easier for parents who have been in harmony with their child because they understand what is going on in their child's mind. They can tailor their approach to discipline to meet their individual child's needs. Discipline focuses on guidance—helping the child learn to do right—rather than on punishing wrongdoing.

Enjoying the child. All these benefits help you enjoy your child more. Helping you enjoy your child is one of the main goals of attachment parenting. When parents and children are in harmony with each other, they do seem to bring out the best in one another. The entire parent-child relationship operates at a higher level. The whole family enjoys being together, and these good feelings help them weather challenges and crises.

Modeling. As you parent your high-need child, you are modeling a style of parenting and interaction that your child will use in future relationships. Parents, keep in mind that you are bringing up someone else's future husband or wife, father or mother. The parenting styles that your child learns from you are the ones he is most likely to follow when he becomes a parent.

How you care for a younger child will also teach older children how to parent. One day my wife and I were sitting in our family room when we heard Erin, then nine months old, crying in our bedroom. Since we believe in responding to our baby's cries, we got up and hurried to the bedroom. As we got near the door, we heard the cries stop. Curious, we looked in to see why Erin had stopped crying, and what we saw left a warm feeling in our hearts: Jim, sixteen at the time, was lying next to Erin, stroking her and gentling her. Why did Jim do this? Because he was following our modeling that when babies cry, someone should listen and respond. Jim is now a dad himself, as well as a pediatrician, and we are pleased and proud of the way he cares for his wife, his children, and his patients. We can't take all the credit, but we know he learned some of this from us.

REFERENCES

Geber, M. 1958. The psycho-motor development of African children in the first year and influences of maternal behavior. *J Soc Psychol* 47:185.

Thomas, A. et al. 1968. *Temperament and Behavior Disorders in Children.* New York: New York University Press.

CHAPTER THIRTEEN

Jonathan: A Case History

This is the story of Jonathan, a thriving high-need child, and his parents Bob and Nancy, who have managed to survive those first difficult years. Nancy tells the story.

"I was so excited to find out I was pregnant. I had 'done my thing' as far as study and travel and now was ready to settle down to raise a family. Generally, my pregnancy was a real joy, but there were periods when I felt ambivalent about having a baby. I had always wanted to have a baby and part of me was excited, but that part was sometimes buried under confusion, anxiety, and an occasional feeling of being trapped. Two years earlier I had suffered a miscarriage, and I was worried it might happen again. It was hard to believe a real baby would result from all of this. I think this all contributed to my feeling inadequate about handling the pregnancy and birth. I felt afraid and powerless.

"Bob and I decided that we needed to be committed to the concept of a family and to each other. We had to dive, as it were, into the whole idea of parenthood, taking it as it came and being willing to sacrifice as necessary. We both made that commitment and to this day we are still involved with it.

"Around the fourth month of my pregnancy, Jonathan started his rumble-tumble act. I knew I had a live wire on my hands, but I didn't realize that all this activity would be so prophetic. I noticed that the baby would respond to sound, physical activity, and my stressful emotions with strong kicking. In fact, if I used the adding machine in the office where I was working, he would kick so hard I had to stop.

"Like many pregnant women, I filled my life with all the baby books I could get my hands on. Bob and I dutifully enrolled in a husband-coached childbirth class and practiced our daily exercises faithfully. As the due date got closer, I became increasingly anxious about the birth. I had read books and seen TV shows where women died in childbirth or sounded as if they were dying. My mother had told me that labor was the most painful, unnatural thing she had ever gone through. I was tired of hearing all those horror stories.

"My labor was traumatic, complicated, and resulted in a cesarean. Bob later confided that because of this medical complication he was initially quite resentful of this little being who had brought his wife so close to disaster. He had to make a conscious effort during the bonding time we had studied and planned for. He knew we would never get those moments back. Even though my delivery did not go as hoped for, I was able to hold Jonathan in the recovery room within a half hour after birth. I began breastfeeding right away and with Bob's help, Jonathan was with me a lot in the hospital as I recovered from the cesarean. Bob and I have since reflected on those first few days of spending time together as a family, and we feel they were vital for our becoming attached to Jonathan and overcoming our disappointment with the traumatic birth.

"Our first night at home was not at all as I had expected. I guess Jonathan decided it was time to begin my training program. I had naively expected to have a feeding schedule as in the hospital, but Jonathan, of course, had other ideas. I couldn't understand why he would not stay asleep when I put him in the crib. Despite my confusion, I was committed to not letting my baby cry, so we spent the night together on the living room couch where I fell asleep sitting up with Jonathan at my breast. When I woke four hours later, I was still sitting in the same position with my baby safe in my arms. I was horrified that I had fallen asleep holding him, but I also worried that he might begin to prefer sleeping with me rather than learning to sleep in his crib. I did not notice the fact that after spending those peaceful hours in my arms, he was calm enough that I could put him in his crib.

"This pattern continued through our first weeks, and I began to realize that Jonathan exhibited more than the normal demands of a newborn. I was baffled at my baby's reluctance to remain alone in his crib and his constant need to nurse. Intellectually I was prepared to breastfeed, but emotionally I was uncertain whether I was willing to sit and nurse all day— and night. Someone told me that tiny babies just ate and slept. My baby just ate. I dreamed of bottles, particularly at night. Jonathan was thriving, but I was languishing. Bob said I was surviving on hormones alone. Breastfeeding honestly did help. It forced me, the compulsive cleaner, to sit down with Jonathan whenever he needed to nurse.

"Besides his non-stop nursing, Jonathan needed non-stop motion. When he was six weeks old, he was no longer content just to lie in my arms. He would not be comforted unless he was being held, carried, rocked, or driven. After Bob came home from work, we took turns walking our son. Bob rocked while I slept. I could not have survived without him.

"My friends kept saying that Jonathan would grow out of it. He didn't. His cries became more intense. I was particularly frustrated by Jonathan's inconsistency in being comforted. What worked one day did not work the next. Some days nothing would satisfy his needs. He did not always find us comforting, but we were better than nothing. I would wonder whether I should give in and pick him up. But while I was thinking, 'Stop screaming and I'll hold you,' Jonathan seemed to be feeling, 'Hold me and I'll stop screaming.' During his clingy times he would look at me as if thinking, 'Do something!' It was a very frustrating situation for me as a parent to be in.

"My training as a teacher in child development kept haunting me. Eric Erickson's stages of social-emotional growth of the child begin with the stage of trust versus mistrust. Jonathan would either learn to trust his environment or learn varying degrees of mistrust. Even if we could not always alleviate Jonathan's discomfort, we could at least hold him and rock him and let him know that we cared. Even if he didn't always settle, he would still be learning trust.

"I felt so tied down. I could do nothing without Jonathan, and no one but me (and Bob when he was home) could care for him. I would get angry with him for being so difficult and then get angry and confused at myself, wondering if I had done something that made him this way. I would oscillate between feeling that I was doing something wrong and knowing that what I was doing was right. For the first time in my life I could understand how someone might abuse a child, and that scared me. My fatigue gave me a short fuse. When Bob got home, boy, did he get it if he stepped out of line! Bob would help calm Jonathan as best he could. I am so grateful that my husband believes in sharing the practical aspects of parenting our children, not just their conception.

"During the first few months I read every book I could find on babies and talked to other mothers and to our pediatrician. I found little information on fussy babies, and much of the advice I found was not right for my baby. By the time Jonathan was four months old, I felt as if I was at the end of my rope. I was angry and tired of reading and hearing that by some magical date he would get over it, sleep through the night, and calm down.

"My friends and relatives seemed equally baffled by Jonathan's behavior. My friends told me to get away from my baby. La Leche League suggested I take him with me. He was too fussy to leave and too fussy to take. Older women, including my mother, innocently suggested that I just put him in his playpen and let him learn to play independently. My milk was often thought to be the culprit. I was so tired of hearing, 'Give him a bottle' and 'Maybe you don't have enough milk.' Some suggested that he had colic, and it would be over by three months. People of the 'cry it out' persuasion and the babysitter-a-week philosophy descended upon us, warning that we were raising a child with terminal dependence who would be unable to grow and make decisions. Worst of all, they told us that Jonathan would be just plain spoiled.

"By now I had become very defensive about my mothering abilities. I was tired of the subtle suggestions that I was causing my baby's fussiness. I knew in my heart that I was a good mother, yet this advice did bother me.

"The biggest lessons Bob and I had to learn were to ignore standard baby advice and to do whatever worked the best at the time, even if it seemed unorthodox. Early on we discarded concepts such as babysitters, weaning at six months, and easily enforced bedtime rituals.

"Once we determined that our rather unorthodox method of raising Jonathan was indeed the course set before us, we wanted others to understand the reasons for our decisions. We learned firsthand, however, that no issue divides adults as quickly as variations in child-raising techniques and philosophies. We learned to pick our friends and supporters carefully. It would have been easier to give in and go along with the standard advice, but our advisors did not know Jonathan. We found the most helpful and affirming advice in the books by William Sears and the most valuable support in our La Leche League Group. It was such a relief to have someone affirm my mothering efforts.

"My greatest enemy in caring for Jonathan during the first year was lack of sleep. Once I discarded the fantasy that he would sleep in his crib and brought him into bed with us, we both slept better. Jonathan and I have fallen into the same sleep pattern. He usually awakens two or three times a night, but now I almost always find myself waking up about thirty seconds before he does. I will then nurse him as soon as he begins to stir, and in a few minutes we both are back to sleep. He is two years old, and this is our usual nighttime pattern.

"Usually I feel rested in the morning and not overly tired during the day. Not all nights are like this, however. Teething pain, separation anxiety, and minor illnesses sometimes throw a wrench into Jonathan's sleep patterns. I've learned that when Jonathan wakes me out of a sound sleep or is awakening four or more times during the night, something is bothering him. Unfortunately, I am not at my most sympathetic at four o'clock in the morning. When I have been up half the night, I have a hard time looking at his feelings instead of my own tired ones. But then, I guess this is a problem that all parents face at times, regardless of where their baby sleeps. Of all the ways to comfort an unhappy baby, I think that lying down and nursing is certainly the easiest. The biggest plus of all is that I really enjoy having Jonathan cuddled up next to me at night. I am so glad that I didn't miss out on this special closeness with him.

"After several good nights in a row, I feel energetic and loving and don't mind devoting most of my time to him. After a few wakeful nights, however, I become resentful, short tempered, and self-pitying. Panicky thoughts invade my mind, 'He's never going to let me have a second baby' or 'This lack of sleep is going to kill me!' Sometimes I just lie there and cry.

"By morning things don't seem quite as bad. When I'm exhausted the best thing to do is simplify my day and concentrate on Jonathan's and my immediate needs. I have learned to ask Bob for help when I am tired—with cooking dinner, for example. It has been a big help when he has offered to take us out for a while, even if it is just for a short walk. I may feel too tired to get out on my own, but having Bob there with us taking charge gives me extra strength.

"I try not to compare Jonathan to other children; it is frustrating to see how much less demanding all my friends' children are. Am I doing something wrong? His needs are so strong and my mothering of him so intense that sometimes I feel as if we are from another planet. Many people cannot understand his needs and the way I respond to them. We are definitely not the average American mother and baby.

"The hidden bomb in this whole scheme of things is the taxing effect this style of parenting has on your marriage. When the child sleeps with you and goes to bed late after an energetic evening, and you have put in long days, day after day, the strain adds up immeasurably. Bob and I both have needs that are not being met. I was converted to the attachment philosophy of parenting almost overnight. Bob, however, took longer to understand why it was so important to Jonathan and me, and there was a lot of tension between us until he did. His support was very, very important to me. I needed someone to protect and defend me while I tended to our baby.

"I also felt guilty about neglecting Bob, but there was very little I could do to change the situation. I was conscious and even sympathetic of Bob's need to have some time and attention from me, but I felt as though I had nothing left over to give to him. This naturally created tension between us, but generally Bob was fairly patient and tried not to put much pressure on me, for which I was grateful. Jonathan was a daily test of our strength and commitment to each other. During the first year, Bob slept on the couch many nights, and we were like ships passing in the night. Jonathan consumed so much time and energy from both of us that we had to schedule any intimate time together."

A Note from Bob

"Overall, I feel that attachment parenting is a positive practice for our family. It is easy to see how well Jonathan responds to it. Since I was raised with a more conventional style of parenting, it took me a little time to go along with it totally. The most obvious frustration for me is a lack of intimacy with my wife. After a full day of mothering Jonathan she is too exhausted. After the close contact with Jonathan all day she seeks out time for herself—time to read, sew, get a long-postponed chore done, or just get some rest. Most of our conversations take place on the run or over the chattering of an enthusiastic two-year-old. My wife and I do enough things with Jonathan that I never really feel left out as a parent. I don't feel the need to compete against my son for Nancy's time either. Despite my frustrations, I truly believe that Jonathan's needs are more important at this time than mine. At two years of age Jonathan is not yet capable of dealing with his frustrations, but I am capable of dealing with mine.

"Jonathan has certainly developed my patience. I am often forced to display amounts of it I never knew I had—not only with Jonathan, but with Nancy, too. The mother of a fussy baby is not always the easiest person to deal with after an especially trying day. Amazingly enough, the sense of commitment toward Jonathan has worked its way into the relationship between Nancy and me. Because we had to go to the bottom of our resources to meet Jonathan's needs, we found a new awareness and respect for each other's strengths. Nancy's willingness to set aside her own needs to nurse Jonathan wherever and whenever had a real impact on me as a father and husband. She gives me inspiration when I feel that too much is being asked of me.

"I can't comfort Jonathan the way Nancy can, but at least I can be supportive of her. While Jonathan reaps the benefits of twenty-four-hour-a-day parenting, nevertheless it should come as a warning that no one can spend that amount of time with a child without experiencing some sort of impatience and frustration. At two years of age Jonathan is still a high-need child.

Because he enjoyed feeling right early on, any deviation from that feeling meets with immediate disapproval."

Back to Nancy

"Things eased up a bit the second year, but life with Jonathan still was not easy. He became happier with each new acquired skill. Walking and talking diffused some of his overabundant energy, and he became a bit more independent of me. He gradually became less of a 'hold me' baby, but still has spent far more time than any baby I know in my arms or in my lap. Weaning is following the same pattern. He is a comparatively frequent nurser, but I see a very gradual tapering off. I still can't help but notice the looks on other people's faces when they see us nursing. Jonathan will probably always be a very sensitive person, but over the past few months he has learned to handle his reactions to sudden sounds and sights better. He remains a very light sleeper.

"What would I say to parents with fussy babies? Listen to your instincts and listen to your baby! I have always assumed that Jonathan cried for a reason, even if I couldn't figure out what it was. The more I followed his cues and my own feelings and observations (instead of others' advice), the easier it became to meet his needs promptly, to help him feel content, and to grow more self-confident as a mother.

"I was once told that a 'good baby' is a baby who cries and lets you know what he needs. That really puts a new perspective on fussy babies—they cry more because they need more!

"One often hears that a family should not change its routines for a new baby—the baby will have to learn to fit in. That just is not true—especially for a high-need baby. For everyone's sanity, the family has to adapt to meet the needs of that baby because the baby doesn't know how to be any different. When Jonathan was born, I never dreamed that he would wind up sleeping in my bed or that I would nurse him for more than two years. Bob never expected to spend some nights on the couch, to cook our breakfast, or occasionally go to a movie by himself. We had to learn to throw out our unrealistic expectations and find ways to meet everyone's needs.

"It takes a certain amount of faith to raise a demanding child. Jonathan is past two, and I often wonder if he will ever sleep through the night, learn to go to sleep without nursing, or view his potty as more than something to stand on. When doubts creep in, I have to remind myself that he learned to walk and talk on his own when he was ready even though I was afraid that because I carried him so much he would never learn to sit up! And he will probably do everything else when he is ready. In other words, if I do my best to meet his needs, he will do his best to grow up."

The Pay-Off

"I can honestly say that having a fussy baby was a blessing. I am glad I was given this type of baby. When he was six months old, I would not have been able to say this, but from the perspective of over two years, looking back at all we have given each other in our relationship, I can see tremendous benefits. Jonathan is growing into a bright, happy, adventurous, and loving child. He is interested in the world around him and is willing to try almost anything as long as Mommy is right there with him. He is kind to others, gentle and loving with babies, and shows an awareness of my feelings. This probably sounds like a mother bragging, but these are all qualities that other people have remarked about. Amazingly the same people who earlier criticized our parenting style now take notice of the results.

"There are some wonderful rewards for putting all that time and energy into a difficult baby. A good example in our case is the subject of discipline. I know Jonathan inside and out and can usually tell what he is thinking. This makes discipline techniques such as verbal instruction, explanation of logical consequences, and modeling (the best of all) very effective tools for teaching him about the world and his place in it. On occasion we must correct Jonathan and dish out negative feedback, but this rarely comes in the form of spanking. Because Jonathan gets so much positive input, the slightest negative response usually does the trick.

"Jonathan is not the only one who is growing. I know I have matured in many ways by caring for him. I think I am more tolerant of other people, and I know I am far more patient and understanding. My confidence in myself not only as a mother but also as a person has greatly increased. Caring for Jonathan has been the greatest effort of my life, and I am more willing now to take on challenges in other areas. I have always tended to plan too far ahead, and Jonathan has taught me the value of flexibility and concentrating on immediate concerns without too much worry toward the future. (At the same time I've learned that it pays to stay one step ahead of him to keep things as smooth as possible.) Providing Jonathan with the intense mothering he has needed has been an extremely satisfying experience for me. It has fulfilled my needs to be creative and to accomplish something tangible and worthwhile. I would never have felt this satisfaction had I left him in the care of someone else and returned to work or school.

"Jonathan has become willing to stay now and then with one of his grandmothers for up to three or four hours. I don't leave him often, but when I do, I explain that I am leaving for a little while and ask if it's all right with him. He acknowledges that he understands and that it is okay. He gives me a hug and reminds me to be back soon. I can see that there is no distress on his part when I leave or return, so that has made me more comfortable about leaving him. Waiting until Jonathan is ready to do something on his own is far more natural and enjoyable for us than an unhappy schedule of pushing him into something too early.

"I must admit that there are times when I miss being the exclusive interest in Jonathan's life, but when one of these moments arises, all I have to do is give him a big hug, and he stops what he is doing and returns it. Mostly, however, I am so proud to see Jonathan growing into a happy, loving, and self-confident little person, especially when I realize that he has done it on his own. I have simply given him the support he needed.

"Seeing the result of hard work is rewarding, of course, but experiencing the close relationship we share is the best pay-off of all. Jonathan and I have gone through a lot together and we both know it. In doing so, we have formed an unbreakable bond of love and understanding, and that is what has made it all worthwhile."

Index

About La Leche League

La Leche League International was founded in 1956 by seven women who wanted to help other mothers learn about breastfeeding. Today La Leche League is an internationally recognized authority on breastfeeding, with a mother-to-mother network that includes La Leche League Leaders and Groups in countries all over the world.

Mothers who contact LLL find answers to their questions on breastfeeding. They also find support from other parents who are committed to being sensitive and responsive to the needs of babies and small children. Local LLL Groups meet monthly to discuss breastfeeding and related issues. La Leche League Leaders are available by telephone and offer information and encouragement for women with questions about breastfeeding.

La Leche League International distributes more than three million publications each year, including many other books by William and Martha Sears. If you have enjoyed The Fussy Baby: How to Bring Out the Best in Your High-Need Child, you will also enjoy NIGHTTIME PARENTING, BECOMING A FATHER, The Baby Book, and The Discipline Book. These and other books by Dr. Sears offer additional information about the philosophy of attachment parenting applied to a multitude of situations.

For more information on breastfeeding, read La Leche League's how-to book, THE WOMANLY ART OF BREASTFEEDING, now in its sixth edition. You'll find more information on nursing past one year of age in MOTHERING YOUR NURSING TODDLER by Norma Jane Bumgarner and HOW WEANING HAPPENS by Diane Bengson.

Look for all these titles in bookstores, or order them from La Leche League International.

- Order publications by phone using your VISA or MasterCard. Call 847-519-9585 or 847-519-7730 weekdays between 9 AM and 5 PM Central Time. Or fax your order to 847-519-0035 or order online at www.lalecheleague.org/

- You can write to LLLI at P.O. Box 4079, Schaumburg IL 60168-4079 USA.

- To find a Leader and an LLL support Group near you, check your local telephone book, or call 1-800-La-Leche or 1-847-519-7730.

- In Canada, call 800-665-4324, or write to LLLC, 18C Industrial Drive, Box 29, Chesterville, Ontario.

- Visit our Web site at www.lalecheleague.org/